Golf Sense

Practical Tips On How To Play Golf In The Zone

Roy Palmer

Illustrated by Sophie Webber

FrontRunner  Publications

Golf Sense: Practical Tips On How To Play Golf In The Zone

Text Copyright © 2010 Roy Palmer
Illustrations Copyright © 2010 Sophie Webber

ISBN 0-956259-30-8
978-0-956259-30-1

Cover design by Sophie Webber
Illustrated by Sophie Webber
Contact: littlestringers@hotmail.com

Layout design by FrontRunner Publications
Book text set in 11pt Palatino Linotype
First published in 2010 by FrontRunner Publications
Contact: roy@play-better-golf.com

Printed and Bound by Lightning Source UK and USA

Acknowledgements

A big thank you to Bob Howard-Spink, who deserves a special mention for painstakingly reading the drafts and testing my techniques on the range. Your help, feedback and advice has been invaluable. And thanks for answering some pretty silly questions with a straight face – questions that only a non-golfer could ask.

Thanks also to Wendy Francis for trying out these procedures out on the course and having the courage to apply them in a competition! Your suggestions on the structure and practical sections have helped make this book easier to follow, and it will hopefully benefit more players as a result.

I would also like to thank all the golfers (and non-golfers) who have endured my experiments and practical sessions and who have read the drafts and made recommendations, including David Balbi, Keith Irving, Bob Mori, Paul Beeson, Alyson Greenstone and Jane Morris.

Special thanks to Andrew Neil from Australia, who took the time to contact me after reading my previous book, *Zone Mind, Zone Body*, to say how it had helped his golf. It was your comments that first planted the thought of writing a book specifically for golfers. Thanks also for reading and letting me know your thoughts on the draft.

A very big thank you to Sophie Webber, who took my stick man pictures and a woolly brief that said make them 'slightly arty and not too anatomical' and who has produced the illustrations throughout this book. More of her work can be seen on her website, not surprisingly called www.sophiewebber.com.

Praise also is due to Angela Sherman whose feedback, encouragement, editing and fine knowledge of grammar have helped to make this book readable.

I wrote most of this book sitting in Frescos Coffee House in Bedford so thank you Kevin and all your staff for providing the brain fuel and not charging me rent!

And, last but not the proverbial least, thanks to my wife, Bernadette, and my children, Tim and Neve, for putting up with me when I haven't been 'in the moment' with them, because I've been preoccupied writing this book.

Contents

Table Of Practical Exercises

Introduction

Are you making your game too complicated? Do you sometimes feel that the more you *try* to get right, the more you get wrong? If all the dos and don'ts are preventing you from enjoying your golf, this book is for you. If, on the other hand, you play like a dream one day while the next day it's the stuff of nightmares, this book is also for you.

Using simple techniques I'll show you how to simplify your golf to become a more consistent player by letting your natural game emerge. Initially these techniques may seem complicated due to the lengthy instructions. However, with practice you'll find you can apply them in a fraction of a second – and they'll make a big difference to your game. You can also download audio instructions from my website; see Useful Resources on page 153.

The techniques I use may also differ from how you've practised before. I place importance on what *not* to do, rather than what you think you need to do. From experience I've found this is the best way to unlearn bad habits that may be preventing you from playing your best golf.

Every player is different, so there's no need to strive to achieve that perfect, one-size-fits-all textbook shot. No two top golfers share the same technique. They're at the top because they've learned how to play to their strengths and make the ball go where they want it to go with a high degree of success. Of course, there are certain cardinal rules that players have discovered over the history of the game, but how you apply these rules may in fact be preventing you playing to your full potential and maybe taking the enjoyment out of your game.

It's common sense that the more you play the better you get. But is it? Have you ever considered whether the hours you put in are productive? Are you over-complicating your game by trying too hard? Do you confuse yourself by attempting to do too much when lining up your shot? I believe in the 'less is more' approach to training. Turn this around and you could think of it as: the more you attempt to do, the more there is to get wrong. Simplify your game and not only will your handicap come down, but you'll also find you learn so much more about golf.

I bet you already have a shelf full of excellent books on technique, golf fitness and how to improve your mental game. But do you have the ability to benefit fully from all this good advice and coaching? I'm not talking about golf skills here, rather a fundamental skill that is the foundation for all learning.

The techniques I use here are easy to apply, regardless of your current golfing ability, and they'll help you get into The Zone – a sublime state where suddenly life and sport don't seem quite so complicated. You may have experienced being in The Zone before, but probably rarely and for only a few fleeting moments. Most of us get into it almost by accident and hence don't know how to get back there again.

Before we go any further I feel I must make a confession. I don't play golf! I've never swung a club in anger, although as a teenager I did get a hole in one at a pitch and putt course. I don't know much about tennis, horse riding, fencing or basketball either, but that hasn't stopped me helping hundreds of players from these sports. I do this by using procedures based on the remarkable system known as The Alexander Technique. It's a technique that will open up a whole new dimension to your game.

This dimension exists in the time between thinking and doing, what I call the 'now moment', and it lasts for only a fraction of a second. What you do in this briefest of moments can undo all of your previous good work. Although you may think you're totally switched on during this vital time, it's quite likely you're unaware of many things you're *actually* doing, due to, paradoxically, your body's process for repeating learned techniques and your efforts to do it right. It's these 'unknowns' that can undermine your endeavours to play good golf and lead to inconsistency. Getting into The Zone heightens your awareness of what you're doing in the 'now moment'. This allows you to reduce considerably those annoying little mistakes you find yourself making, in spite of knowing you shouldn't, plus quite a few more you may not be aware of.

I hope to encourage a subtle shift in your approach to golf that will dramatically change your understanding of what underpins your performance. I can show you how to develop a new skill or, as I see it, a new sense: a *golf sense* that will get you into The Zone more often and take your game to the next level.

1 Birdies And Butterflies

Few people are better qualified to talk about chaos theory than golfers. One moment you're playing a shot like a pro and the next... Well let's not go there. With so many variables involved, the slightest move at the wrong time can put you in the rough, in a bunker or stranded somewhere up that unpleasant creek without a paddle. When it comes to sporting techniques there surely can't be one that has been analysed, agonised over, reinvented or written about more than the golf swing; and I bet the putt comes in a close second.

A golfer at the top of their game is a beautiful sight to behold, as science, art and skill combine to achieve what logically appears almost impossible. A thought creates a chemical reaction, translates into a billion electrical pulses, activates around 700 muscles and 206 bones to perform a miracle of coordination, organisation and implementation to achieve an expectation. If you tried to catalogue each and every single action in this brief moment it would take months, but you can do it in a second.

When it works well, it feels so simple and immensely satisfying. When it doesn't, it feels like each part of your body is doing its own thing in conflict with every other part. You might begin to wonder if you'll ever be capable of doing it again.

So why the difference? What works so well one moment and not the next?

It only takes a tiny amount of inappropriate activity in one seemingly insignificant muscle to upset your rhythm and fluff the shot. Unfortunately, the majority of us simply don't have the degree of sensitivity or self-awareness to notice the small differences from one shot to the next.

Let's look at one of the many variables that can affect the outcome of your swing.

Do you stiffen your neck just before you swing? Do you know? If you have the habit of tightening your grip on the club handle, this can also cause your neck and jaw muscles to tighten. It's probably not on your list of things to do, but I see many golfers doing it in preparation. Does it matter?

If you unknowingly tighten your neck or clench your jaw just before you swing, it changes the dynamics of your swing. I say 'unknowingly' because, as we'll see shortly, you may be employing any number of unnecessary actions when you move and yet be completely unaware of them.

What other people may find in poetry or art museums, I find in the flight of a good drive.
Arnold Palmer

On Monday you may tighten slightly with no noticeable effect on the shot, whereas on Tuesday you may do it a fraction more and see the ball go wayward. If you're not aware that you're doing this in the first place, it becomes an unknown variable in your technique and leads to an inconsistency with no obvious cause. More importantly, if you don't know you're doing it, you can't control it.

Throughout this book there are experiments and exercises that allow you to put the theory to the test. These will be easier if you can get a colleague to read them to you or, alternatively, you can download audio instructions available from my website – see Useful Resources on page 153.

Playing In The Zone [1] – *The Chair*

For starters we'll have a look at an everyday action away from golf to demonstrate what I mean by 'unknown variables'. You may wonder what this practical exercise has to do with golf, but please bear with me and all will become clear.

 This simple exercise can reveal some interesting things about how you move.

1) Sit on a chair and get ready to stand up.

2) Ask yourself what you do to get ready. Do you do any of the following?

   • Put your hands on your legs or chair

   • Pull in your lower back

   • Push your chest forward

   • Pull your head back

   • Hold your breath

   • Lift your shoulders

   • Make a noise as you get up

3) Ask someone to watch and tell you what you do.

You'll need someone to observe because you may do some of these things but not notice. Actually, I'm willing to bet my house against yours that you'll do at least one of them. The actions I mention above will actually interfere with your reflexes for coordinating movement by adding something extra *before* you've even moved. Some of your muscles are working when they shouldn't be, while others are inactive when they should be assisting. In short, you're making the movement much harder than it should be.

Fig 1.1 If you're one of the many people who do one or more of the actions mentioned above, you're actually making this everyday movement harder than it should be!

So what's how I get out of a chair got to do with my golf? The important points to consider here are:

Why were you unaware of the additional effort and actions you used before they were brought to your attention?

Why do you do them if they're inefficient?

Why does it still feel right to do it like this?

Are you aware of any such actions in your technique?

You can go a long way to improving your game by developing your skills of self-awareness and focus. Thankfully, nature appears to have given us a solution, one that I believe was originally developed for improving our chances of survival in a hostile world. It's also pretty useful on the golf course.

Easy Does It

Think back to the best shot you've ever played. It doesn't matter if it was twenty minutes or twenty years ago, you can probably recall every minor detail with ease. Perhaps it was a hole in one, a miraculous shot out of the bunker or the mother of all putts to take the game at the last hole. Executing the perfect shot gives you a high that may even rank up there with your wedding day – although it's probably best to keep that to yourself!

How did it feel? Did you put a lot of effort into that shot? No? It was one of the easiest shots you've ever played, wasn't it? Ask all the golfers you know and they'll describe a similar sensation: it's as if the shot played itself. Everything just flowed as your wish became your command, and your body, club and ball did exactly what you asked them to do. Was there indecision? Or a long debate on how you were to play the shot? No? Golfers recounting their perfect moment to me have said definitely not. Although they all could recall the situation, conditions and outcome, when they came to describe what it felt like, they used words such as 'instinctive', 'flowing', 'light' and 'easy'. Note the absence of technical terms.

This experience is what athletes refer to as 'The Zone'; artists and writers call it 'The Flow'. You temporarily existed in a different state with a heightened sense of awareness. Everything seemed easier and simpler, and you instinctively knew exactly what you had to do – nothing more, nothing less. With little perceived effort you played a peach of a shot worthy of a story years later for your grandchildren. Suddenly there were no more unknowns or parts of your body doing their own thing. You became an integrated, coordinated and uncomplicated golfer, able to execute your intentions with greater ease.

This is probably why you play golf. Of course it's good to win or lower your handicap, but to experience one of these perfect moments can even surpass the trophies. However, one of the frustrations of playing any sport is varying form. Wouldn't it be great if we could enter The Zone at will or, at the very least, experience it more often? Athletes I've interviewed from all sports have expressed both mild annoyance and extreme frustration at not knowing what they did to get into The Zone. Suddenly they're in it and the next moment they're back out of it and unable to return. I believe this is a clue.

The fact that we can unexpectedly find ourselves in The Zone without knowing how we got there suggests there's an 'automatic' or subconscious element involved somewhere in the process, so perhaps we shouldn't try. Through experience I've found the best way into The Zone is to remove the inhibitors such as anxiety, concentrating too hard and one other factor we'll examine shortly: habit. Take these out of the equation, play your sport and let nature run its course.

Habits or conditioned reflexes that allow us to repeat tasks with almost no thought can work for us or very much against us, especially when it comes to achieving a peak performance. In the next chapter we'll look at how your habits can stop you getting into the sublime state of The Zone – and ironically it's something you feel you *should* be doing.

2 Doing The Right Thing?

Do you make mistakes in your game? Of course you do. Everyone does. Obviously the harder the shot the more chance there is for error, but what about those infuriating mistakes on a straightforward one you really know you shouldn't miss? Have you ever considered that it's because you're trying to get it right? Yes, it sounds ridiculous, but in many cases it's true.

Let's imagine you have a two-yard putt to sink. You've done it many times before, but this time it all goes horribly wrong and you end up further away from the hole than when you started. Maybe in your mind you've played the perfect shot – it was just for the wrong hole!

It's very easy to be wise after the event, and I'm sure your buddies will quickly point out where they think you went wrong, but did you mean to play it like that? You didn't deliberately play to miss and you probably did everything that felt right in your preparation, so why the error?

If your putt does go horribly wrong, it's because that's how you told yourself to play it. Your actions caused your body to do it *exactly* that way! The ball ends up a country mile away from the hole because that's where you put it – the evidence is irrefutable. Somewhere between your intention and the execution something happened. What came out at the end of the chain did not resemble what you thought you'd put in at the start.

There are two possible explanations:

1) You incorrectly judged the conditions and the green, so what you thought needed to be done was just plain wrong and consequently you played the wrong shot.

2) You correctly judged what was needed and in your mind you worked out and played the right shot, but your body didn't *appear* to do what you wanted.

In (1) this comes down to experience. The more you play the better able you are to read the green and judge the weight and back swing required to the make the ball go the distance in varying conditions – although you may have already discovered this can change from day to day. Other factors will affect the outcome, such as the green didn't play as it looked or there's a sudden gust of wind or another unforeseen circumstance. But that's the beauty of the game! It would get a bit dull if these random factors weren't a part of it. We have to accept that there are things beyond our control. So let's focus on what we *can* control.

In (2) I say 'appear' because your body can only do what you tell it to do. The trick is to know *what* you're telling your body to do. When you concentrate on getting it right, you may unwittingly be doing far more than you're aware of and hence undermine your ability to execute each shot as intended.

The outcome of each shot relies on:

1) How you read the situation

2) How you've played a similar shot before

3) How well you put your plan into action

4) Unknown factors

Although I have previously said that most unknown factors are beyond your control, there are still ways you can reduce their impact. It's only an unknown factor if you haven't taken it into account.

Gorillas In Our Midst

I take pride in my observational skills, although my wife may beg to differ, but I was caught out by an excellent demonstration on just how much we can miss when we focus on one thing. When watching a video made by researchers at The University of Illinois, I was asked to count how many times the ball was passed between the players in a basketball team. Easy enough I thought, so I followed the ball avidly and got the correct answer. Yet when asked to watch the same clip again without counting, I saw a man dressed as a gorilla walk into the middle of the court and wave at the camera for a few seconds before walking off! You can see another version of this video on my website. See useful resources on page 153.

Because this wasn't relevant to my task the first time round, I completely missed it. My eyes picked up the image and sent it to the visual centres of my brain but, because it wasn't important, it didn't get the attention of my conscious mind. Our selective awareness doesn't apply just to vision. How many things are you doing unknowingly with your muscles that could be seriously affecting your technique?

I assume you rarely see gorillas on the golf course, but how can you judge what is and what isn't pertinent to the shot if your focus is too narrow? Bear in mind that from day to day your level of awareness will vary. External unknown factors are one aspect to consider, but you may be surprised to learn there are also internal unknowns influencing your game. These are the things you're doing with your body that can ruin your shot, yet you're blissfully unaware as to why. If you're responsible for them, they really shouldn't be an unknown part of the equation.

When Two Wrongs *Can* Make A Right

Think back to *The Chair* practical exercise on page 15 and how you used a number of unnecessary actions to complete the movement. How about the preparation and execution of your swing? Could there be anything you're doing here that's stopping your body flowing as freely as it could? I'll assume that you'll spend more time on your shot than contemplating getting out of a chair, but the principal remains the same. In fact, you could be doing even more unnecessary actions that are detrimental to your swing. Why the ball goes straight down the fairway one day and not the next could be due to the intensity of one of these hidden actions.

 Try this, I think you might find this interesting:

1) **Fold your arms.**

2) **See which arm you have on the outside.**

3) **Now fold them the opposite way.**

4) **How does that feel? How long did it take?**

Did you have to stop and think about how to fold them the other way around? When you eventually got there did it feel wrong? There's nothing wrong about the opposite way, but would you choose to fold your arms like that normally? Of course you wouldn't.

Firstly, folding your arms is usually a subconscious action, so you'll automatically do it without thinking. Secondly, you wouldn't do it if it felt wrong. You wouldn't do anything in a way that felt wrong, whether it's absent-mindedly getting up from a chair, folding your arms or preparing to play a vital shot. It would throw you completely off your stride if you suddenly felt something unusual or out of the ordinary when doing something you've done one hundred thousand times before. Yet, while you continue to do things in the 'right' way, you're severely limiting your potential to improve your game because you're at the mercy of your habits.

If you always do something in the same habitual way, you have nothing to compare your technique against.

This is a vital concept to understand. When we come to look at improving your technique or trouble-shooting, you'll see that most people start the process too far down the line. How you prepare both mentally and physically is also susceptible to habit. In my book, *Zone Mind, Zone Body*, I talk about 'The Matrix Triangle' – the three factors that determine the boundaries and rules for how we perform. These are: conditioning, concept and habit. Do something often enough in a particular way and you're programming yourself to always do it that way. When looking to improve your game, it's worth considering Einstein's wise words: "Insanity is doing the same thing over and over again and expecting different results."

Whether you use visualisation, sports psychology, traditional training techniques or decidedly unconventional methods, when it comes down to the moment you play the shot, your old habits will happily take control in a flash. These rarely change and will invariably be done in the same way regardless of how you prepare. Habits remain the foundation for everything you do, regardless of how you intend to do it. Unless, that is, you can change what happens in the fraction of a second before you act.

Of course, habits can work to your advantage if you've perfected the stroke, but if we're honest with ourselves, how often is this the case? Besides, there is a danger that an 'automatic' skill can be lost following an injury or if you start to add something new to your technique. To be capable of doing something well, and to know *why* you can do it well, is immensely satisfying and is a safeguard against injury if you know how to consciously recreate it time after time.

What feels right only feels right because you're familiar with the sensation. If something feels wrong in your preparation, it's because you don't normally do it that way. There may be nothing wrong with the new way at all. In fact it could be more right than your habitual way! So why not try it sometime? In the privacy of your own home have a go at a simple putt and do something different that you wouldn't normally consider. Don't try to 'get it right'. In fact, don't give a fig about getting it right – and see what happens. See the practical exercise at the end of this chapter.

The next time you're preparing to play a shot, think about how you decide whether you're doing it right? Well, obviously you only have one way of judging whether it is right – by how it *feels*. But wait a minute! You've just discovered with the arm-folding experiment that what feels right is purely down to habit, because that's all you've ever known.

I wanted you to do the arm-fold early on, because the sensation you felt in the second part is what I want you to experience when trying the procedures in this book. If it feels a little odd or unfamiliar, it means you're doing it differently – that is, not using your old habits. For our purposes that's a good thing. You'll be doing something new, which gives you the opportunity to compare it with your old technique and determine what works for you.

Trying *not* to get it right also helps to increase your awareness of every action you're doing. When you try to get it right and trust the old habits, you can drift into autopilot, practically switch off and miss many pertinent actions that make up your shot – just like all those things you may have been doing to get out of a chair.

If a fly lands on your forearm as you're preparing to swing, you'll instantly become aware of its presence on your skin. This is because it's a new sensation, and your nervous system notifies your conscious mind that something unexpected has just occurred.

However, all of the other sensations coming from your muscles can be virtually ignored, because it's business as usual and you're comfortably familiar with them. Even if your muscles are pulling your shoulders up around your ears, your nervous system won't bother to let you know because it associates these sensations with your technique.

Reverse every natural instinct and do the opposite of what you are inclined to do, and you will probably come very close to having a perfect golf swing.

Ben Hogan

So if you rely on the feeling of 'rightness' as a guide for your preparation, you're actually preventing yourself from noticing many parts of your technique. You're removing them from your control and stopping yourself getting into the right frame of mind to enter The Zone.

Let's look at this concept in a practical situation.

Tom's Predicament — Part One

Throughout the book we're going to follow a semi-pro called Tom as he struggles with a problem that's affecting his swing. We'll see how he can use a non-golfing approach initially to identify the cause, and how he can start to overcome the problem before he's even picked up his club. He could use the same process for addressing any problem with his game.

Tom has started to hook the ball off the tee, whereas previously the ball went straight down the fairway more often than not. Once he started to compete at a more senior level stress became a factor, resulting in a small but unperceivable amount of tension in his neck and shoulders. Gradually this tension became part of his technique because it *felt right*. So now he will unconsciously prepare for his shot by tightening the neck and shoulders in anticipation of the swing. He won't start to play until everything feels in place. It's a bit like revving your car's engine before pulling away from the lights.

The first indication Tom has of the problem is the obvious outcome of the ball landing in the rough and *not* the feeling of tension, because this is now an automatic habit and therefore ignored. Tom knows something is wrong and will try to alter his swing. But his attempts to correct the problem start too far down the chain. He's focusing on the preparation and execution of the act – and not on how he *prepares* to prepare, that is, to stiffen his neck and shoulders slightly. This feeling is his template or foundation for the technique. He won't be aware of the tension because it's there before he's conscious that he's getting ready to play.

However, Tom's attempts to correct the problem only complicate matters further. The harder he concentrates on getting it right, the more he tightens his neck and shoulders – because his feeling of what is right demands this. Other changes he makes to his swing will take him further away from his previously natural swing, because they are now built on top of the suspect foundation. So the more he tries to be right, the more he will rely on his familiar but unreliable habit of getting set for the shot.

His confidence takes a nosedive because he can no longer trust his judgment or his ability to make adjustments. In his own mind he's doing the right thing, yet if he's oblivious to these actions in his technique, he can't change them.

Things get worse when he seeks the help of a coach who sees Tom raising his shoulders and instructs him not to do it. Now his confidence in his ability is further dented as he's told not to do something that feels right. When he tries to carry out what he's been told to do, it will feel wrong (remember your reaction to the opposite arm-fold) and he'll start to believe he doesn't know anything about golf.

So how can Tom break his dependency on trusting his habits and trying to do the right thing all the time? He has to relearn a skill he had as a two-year old – one that unfortunately he's spent most of his life trying hard to lose.

We'll come back to see how Tom's getting on throughout the rest of the book.

Playing In The Zone [2] — *To Putt Or Not To Putt*

Before you can get in The Zone you need to break free of the habits that drag you down the same path every time you prepare to play. Whether they contribute positively to your technique or not, the act of focusing on *exactly* what you're doing to prepare will expose many of those previously unknown variables that can ruin your shot. If you're gliding along on autopilot you'll miss more than you think. Remember, what you want to do only feels right because you've done it this way thousands of times before.

 Have a go at this exercise now, before reading the next chapter:

1) Place a plastic cup, or whatever object you use to aim at when practising in your home or office, on the floor and put the ball a reasonable distance away so it's not too easy.

2) Line up the shot and then get ready to play the shot.

3) Observe what you feel you have to do next before you start the putt.

4) Perhaps you want to tighten your grip a fraction, jiggle the club, wiggle in your stance or hold your breath. You may have a few more of your own to add to this list.

5) Do you need to do any of these? Do they help with your shot?

6) Now start over again and see if you can take the putt without doing any of your usual actions, even if you think they're necessary.

7) If you feel you're about to do one of your usual preparations, stop, and start again.

8) Don't be concerned about whether you hit the target with your putt.

If you found it difficult to *not* do what you felt necessary, don't worry, we'll be using more techniques to help you overcome this later. This is the first step to taking greater control over your actions and becoming a more consistent player.

3 Being In The Moment

Have you ever met one of those really annoying people who seem able to play any sport of their choosing with little or no coaching? They pick up a club one day and within a ridiculously short space of time they're better than you'll ever be. To make things worse they don't even appear to have to try, or even realise just how good they really are. How can they do that? What have they got that you haven't?

Regardless of the sport, your success depends on a set of basic skills that form the foundation you're going to build upon. These skills include the usual suspects such as hand-eye coordination, balance, strength, suppleness and stamina, plus your mental capacity for concentration, observation and application. But there is another one, one that is fundamental to the others, and yet very few people give it a thought. When I tell you what it is you'll probably think *'Is that all?'* It doesn't sound much, or even that exciting, but it's immensely powerful; it's an ability to 'be in the moment'.

When you're in the moment, it's as if every action is a deliberate, carefully-thought-out response to the task in hand, yet with little perceived effort. You're totally focused and in control, allowing your training, experience and skill to combine to produce that near perfect shot. When you're out of it, you only see half the picture and your body seems unable to do what you ask of it.

Our irritating friend, Mr Perfect, has this ability in spades and probably doesn't even know it because he's always had it. While we mortals struggle to reach our destination with a muddy windshield and no map, his car is spotless and has the benefit of satellite navigation. It's no surprise that he can pick things up so quickly.

Yet we all had this ability once. When we were toddlers we lived in the moment, as we had little perception of places and events away from our immediate surroundings. A miserable child can be taken from one moment to a completely different place with a simple, *"Wow, look at that over there"* or *"What have I got in my hand?"* Diverting attention away from the present difficulty onto something else that's new and interesting can instantly change the mood of a child, and even a frustrated golfer!

Being in the moment has huge benefits for golfers. Sports psychologist, Michael Lardon, believes successful sports people are where they are because, amongst other things, they've developed a skill he calls 'instant amnesia'. This allows them to 'let go' of a mistake and not let it affect their next move. Once each phase of the game is complete, they can move on to the next and play each shot as if it was their first of the day.

I see being 'in the moment' as the first step to getting into The Zone; you suddenly step up to a gear you didn't know you had. So, all you need to do is to get into the moment and then wait for the rest to happen. It sounds easy enough, doesn't it? Yet, due to our fast-paced lives and the nature of our conditioning, the moments we spend in the 'here and now' are rare. We invariably spend most our time well out of it. The old adage is true – we spend all morning at the office talking golf and all afternoon on the course talking business. Our minds wander from the task we've set ourselves, race too far ahead, or worse still concentrate so hard on what we're trying to do that we miss the most obvious things.

This ability to live from moment to moment allows you to break the dependence on habits that may be choking your technique. If you're lacking in this skill, or at best it's erratic, the heights you reach in golf will be limited. You'll eventually reach a level where further progress seems beyond you. It doesn't seem to matter how much extra coaching or practice you have, you appear to make very little progress. So, instead of banging your head against that brick wall, why not take a step back and look around for the gate. It's a lot easier.

 Let's see if we can get into this moment with this simple experiment:

1) **Touch the end of your nose with your finger.**

2) **So far, so good.**

3) **Now rest the same hand on your leg and think about how you're going to do it again. In your mind see your hand and arm moving and 'feel' it touch your nose.**

4) **Think about moving your hand but don't let it move just yet.**

5) **Now let you hand rise from your leg and be aware of its movement through the air towards your nose and then make contact with it.**

Okay, I know this isn't exactly exciting stuff and I doubt it will ever be up there competing with the thrill of a round of golf, but it is relevant. We're interested in the difference between the first and second time of doing the same act. The first time you'll have probably switched off between starting the movement and the end part of touching your nose. You're not in the moment. You've been given a task to do and the bit in between is irrelevant. It's the final part of making contact with the end of your nose that's important.

The second time you're being asked to think about the movement before and during the act, and so you maintain your focus throughout. You're in the moment. You may also have had a different sensation in the second part of how much time it took to complete, because you were aware of much more happening while doing it.

The greater level of awareness of the act allows you more control, as you could stop or alter the movement of your arm at any time. If you've switched off during the movement, waiting for the end part to happen, you don't have this luxury. The difference is down to how you prepared for the movement the second time, and where you placed your attention, that is, not on the end but at the start, maintaining it for the whole act.

Playing In The Zone [3] – ***Getting Into The Moment***

 Please try the following practical exercise without a ball:

1) Take a putter in your hands and stand so you're ready to go into your stance – but don't move just yet.

2) First you need to get to a quiet place in your mind to reduce undue muscular activity. One that works for me is to imagine an orchestra tuning up, I then hear the conductor tap his baton on the rostrum, followed by silence. You don't have to use this particular routine but you'll need something that prompts you to come to a still, quiet state.

3) If you're more of a visual person, you could visualize a pond with a few ripples slowly working their way across the surface until it's completely still.

4) To immerse yourself in the moment, place your awareness on something relevant to the situation. It doesn't have to be anything clever. Here are a few *getting into the moment thoughts*. You may think of a few more, but it has to be something not directly related to your technique – and something that doesn't take you away from the moment like the price of fish!

    •   Your toes in your socks

    •   The ground under your feet

    •   The touch of your clothes on your skin

    •   The light touch of your lips upon each other

    •   The movement of your ribs against your clothes

    •   The sounds around you

5) Maintain awareness of one or two of the above and release into your stance.

6) Notice the movement of air going in and out of your nose.

7) Sense the contact of all parts of your hands on and around the club handle.

8) Move your club like a pendulum gently to and fro while focusing on your breathing and hands.

The objective is to be aware of all of your actions while moving your club. This will help you improve control of your putter and prevent sudden jerky actions.

4 Minding The Gap

In the introduction I talked about opening up a 'whole new dimension' to your game. Yes, it may sound a bit dramatic, but when you realise just how much more you can control by being in the moment, I think you'll agree it's justified. I could have also used the term 'creating a window of opportunity', because you'll sense having more time to think things through before you act.

I'm sure you're familiar with Pavlov's experiment involving dogs and bells. Dogs salivate when food is placed in front of them. Humans also do this, but thankfully it's less noticeable. Pavlov rang a bell a few minutes before feeding time, and before long the dogs began to associate the sound of the bell with eating and therefore began to dribble when it rang. These are conditioned reflexes, more commonly known as habits, because it's a learned behaviour. Tom's habit of lifting his shoulders is a conditioned reflex. If you've learned to do it, even if unknowingly, it's possible to learn not to do it. But first you have to recognise you're doing it.

The main problem with these habits is they're triggered without any conscious effort on our behalf. Tom doesn't consciously choose to lift his shoulders to prepare, and therefore he cannot choose *not* to lift them yet. These habits remove large parts of your technique from your conscious control. This, of course, can be beneficial if it's a good habit because certain parts of your technique can take care of themselves. However, even this can work against you if, due to something like an injury or a crisis of confidence, you lose it. If you no longer have that knowledge at a conscious level, you'll struggle to get it back.

In Pavlov's experiment, the bell was the stimulus that brought about the response of salivating. On the golf course, you're bombarded by stimuli such as the tee, the ball, your club, the flag and your playing partners. The very thought of hitting the ball will evoke a chain reaction, including many actions you may no longer notice. To prevent these habitual actions, you need to prevent the first link in the chain reaction, that is, the thought of getting set to hit the ball. However, scientific research has found you have very little time to do this. The next time your telephone rings, see if you can consciously make the decision to answer it or leave it *before* you start to move. Pavlov's dogs would have been hard-pressed to respond to the bell quicker than most humans respond to their phones ringing.

The Reality Gap

What you want to happen on the golf course and what actually happens are often two very different things. I refer to this as 'the reality gap'. Once you learn how to master getting into the moment, the narrower this gap will become. A client of mine refers to this as 'increasing the range of his radar'. It happens as he becomes more aware of the seemingly small unnecessary actions that he's bringing to his game. Previously, whether he did these or not was something left to chance.

When an element of chance exists in your game there is inconsistency and, as you're probably only too well aware, this can ruin a good game.

The split second just *before* you act can be the make or break for your game. This is the gap you have to mind to reduce the discrepancy between your intention and the outcome. We'll look at this from a practical point of view in the next chapter. For now here's the science – plus an interesting experiment with habits.

The Science Of The Moment

Experiments into human consciousness and movement in the early 1980s by Dr. Benjamin Libet, a professor of physiology, concluded that, "There are 300 to 350 milliseconds within which a person may either prevent or allow an urge to move to become an action". What does this mean? When your phone rings, if you don't consciously make a decision within a third of a second after hearing the tone, your habitual reaction kicks in and you'll be reaching for it before you've had chance to decide whether you were going to answer it or not.

His next discovery exposed the weird and wonderful nature of a habit and questioned our rather comforting notion of being in control, in other words, having free will. Libet measured neural activity sending signals to muscles *before* his subjects had consciously decided to move. He suggested that this activity in the brain happens before any conscious thought. He also suggested that it may even lead us to do things that we believe we have chosen to do for ourselves, whereas, in fact, we'd acted before we'd had chance to think it through. Is this ringing any bells? Ever had this sort of experience on the green?

The thought that we may not have control over any number of our actions may sound unbelievable; after all it does have its origins in San Francisco during the swinging 60s, but have you ever entered a room and suddenly thought, 'N*ow what did I come in here for?*' This is a perfect example of not being in the moment and of allowing yourself to react without any conscious thought on your behalf. You're happily daydreaming away when suddenly you find yourself doing something – and you have no recollection as to why.

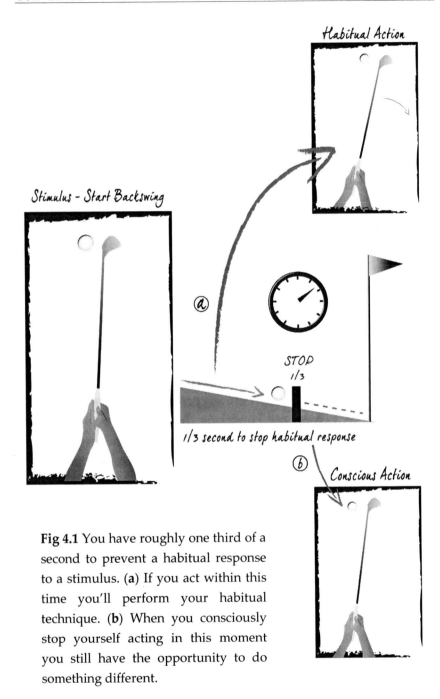

Habitual Action

Stimulus - Start Backswing

(a)

STOP
1/3

1/3 second to stop habitual response

(b)

Conscious Action

Fig 4.1 You have roughly one third of a second to prevent a habitual response to a stimulus. (**a**) If you act within this time you'll perform your habitual technique. (**b**) When you consciously stop yourself acting in this moment you still have the opportunity to do something different.

Only the other day, I suddenly found myself walking into my office and standing at the filing cabinet wondering what I was doing there. Did I make the conscious decision to be there? No. To figure out what I was doing there, I had to play back in my head what I was thinking previously. I realised I'd heard something on the radio that triggered the thought that I needed to send a letter – and before I knew it I was looking for an envelope in the cabinet.

Unfortunately, it seems to happen more often with age, and I believe it's because we spend less and less time in the moment. If I had been practising what I preach, I would have registered the stimulus from the radio, consciously decided that I still needed to post the letter, and then I'd have chosen whether to do it straight away or save it for later when I'd finished my current task.

Libet's research uncovered another no-less-remarkable discovery. He found that our experience of when a movement starts *precedes* the moment our muscles contract to carry out the act. So while the muscles are ready and willing to go before we're consciously aware, we also get a sense that we're moving before we actually do it!

What does this all mean? Am I really hitting that ball or did someone just pull my strings?

Since 1999, further studies by Patrick Haggard and Martin Eimer have discovered why this may be the case. They found that, before we move, information about our position and situation is fed into the part of our brain that simulates our intended movement and works out what it's going to feel like. This simulation is then compared with previously stored patterns of similar such movements, and any differences between the predicted and stored patterns are corrected in favour of the stored model. So even if you know there's something wrong with your technique, your brain would still rather stick with what it already knows!

43

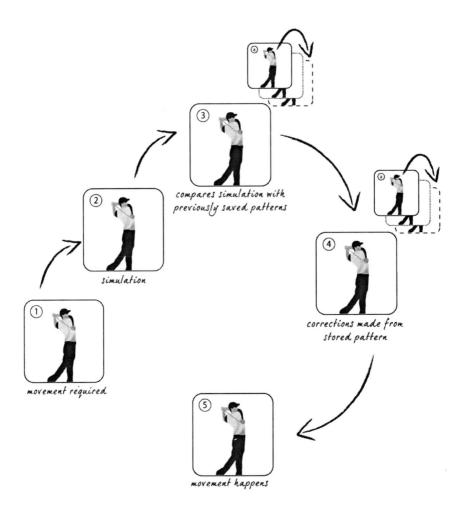

Fig 4.2 The movement selection process. (1) We receive a stimulus to move. (2) Our brain works out what is required and how it's going to feel. (3) and (3a) Comparisons are made with stored patterns of similar movements. (4) and (4a) Differences between the simulation and stored patterns are corrected in favour of the stored pattern. (5) The chosen stored pattern is executed. In other words, your habitual way of performing the movement is the most likely outcome.

Other studies appear to back this up. Research found that experts in a particular skill produce more rapid corrections in the planning stage, compared to novices in the same skill – because the experts have a larger portfolio of actions with which to make comparisons. So, in effect, your brain is keen to reproduce your familiar 'tried and tested' technique.

This is great if your technique is perfect, but not so great if it's not. If you've done it poorly a few thousand times before, there's a higher probability that you'll do it that way again. In other words, you can get better at doing it badly.

> 66
> *In the beginner's mind there are many possibilities, but in the expert's there are few.*
> Shunryu
> Suzuki-Roshi
> 99

In the beginner's brain there are more possibilities, because they have yet to develop a 'tried and tested' habitual technique that's become hard-wired in their brain. Beginners usually have lower expectations and less invested in the shot, and so they tend not to get anxious or distracted by trying to get it right.

The ideal golfer would have the approach of a beginner, that is, be open to experimenting and free from anxiety about the outcome, as well as having the accuracy and application of an expert.

To Do Or Not To Do

When you tried *The Chair* exercise on page 15 you probably found you performed a number of unnecessary actions. Yet, if you try to get up without doing them, you'll find it quite a challenge. This is because your brain has already decided what it's going to tell your muscles to do – before you've even started to move.

So how can you take real control over your actions? Have a go at the exercise on the next page.

Can you stop your brain dictating what you do?

1) **Sit at the edge of your chair.**

2) **Think about getting up.**

3) **See what preparations you make to get up.**

4) **Now try to get up *without* those preparations.**

Once you've decided to get up, your muscles are all set and ready to go. If you do this movement consciously, as opposed to unconsciously, then when you get up to answer the telephone for example, you're able to exert a greater degree of control. If you still find step 4 (above) difficult, it's because you're still thinking of doing the same movement. In other words, you're still thinking about getting up from a chair.

To change this pattern you need to think of *not* getting up from a chair.

This may seem slightly bizarre advice, but this way you can prevent your habitual pattern being selected for the task and automatically firing signals to your muscles. This gives you the freedom to try something different. It would be very difficult, if not impossible, to stop the unnecessary actions you make in step 3 (the output) without changing what you're thinking (the input).

So how can you get up from a chair without thinking of getting up from a chair?

You break it down and think of one stage at a time, just as you probably did when you first learned to swing and putt. By now, the individual components of your technique are bundled up and stored in the lower levels of your brain, ready to be activated by a single thought. However, blind reliance on this habit can prevent you from noticing the less-than-efficient movements that may have crept in over the years. Focusing on each stage in turn brings more actions back to your awareness and consequently under your control. It also conveniently gets you into the moment.

 Now have a go at getting up from the chair again, but think of the following:

1)   **Let your head lead your torso over your feet.**

2)   **Feel your weight go into the floor and let your knees come back.**

3)   **Your legs will straighten and you'll be standing up.**

Alternatively, you can think of 'falling up' out of the chair.

Fig 4.3 By *not* getting set to stand, your reflexes are able to coordinate the movement unimpeded.

When you break down the movement and stay focused on the individual parts, you won't race ahead of yourself. You'll stay in the moment and at no time will you need to think of standing up. To think of the movement in a different way can 'fool your brain' about what you're going to do next. If you let the cat out of the bag too soon, all your habitual actions will be active in a flash – and you've missed the chance to do it another way.

This is just one example using an everyday movement. On the golf course you'll be surprised at just how quickly your game will improve once you learn how to use this gap between thinking and doing. Previous unknown actions adversely affecting your technique, similar to those unnecessary preparations you made to get up from a chair, will jump out at you. It's like switching off the cacophony of conflicting signals racing around your body and being able to hear the symphony for the first time.

Use The Force

Coordination is a key component for generating maximum power at the right time for your swing. Professor Robin Sharp, at the University of Surrey, calculated which parts of the upper body should be used for the swing and, more importantly, at what stage. His study suggests that the wrists are not as important as once believed and that it's the use of the arms that has a greater influence. Sharp believes the best results are achieved by increasing the power of rotation to a maximum shortly after starting the swing and then maintaining this force throughout.

He says, "Generating too much arm speed too soon causes an early release, with the club-head reaching its maximum speed before it arrives at the ball." To achieve the optimal power he suggests, "Hitting first with the shoulders while holding back with the arms and wrists and, after some delay, hitting through with the arms."

Successful execution to this degree of accuracy requires strength, coordination and sensitivity. Strength is important, but it's about as useful as a rudderless boat if you don't have the ability to control it. If you can't sense what's happening during the technique, you won't be able to control and prevent the unwanted actions. However, the more you attempt to control your actions, the greater the chance of getting it wrong. So perhaps doing less means there's less chance to duff the shot. Think back to your best shot again (as if you need any encouragement) and ask yourself just how much control you felt you had to exert over that one.

When you're in The Zone the shots are so much easier!

If you've played the perfect shot, even if only once, you'll know it's within you to do so; it's just that your efforts to repeat it are getting in the way. Effort involves doing something more on top of what's required, adding unnecessary muscle actions to your technique and interfering with coordination. If your preparation includes tightening your neck and shoulders, your sensitivity – and hence your control – will be drastically reduced.

Your neck muscles play a vital role in coordinating movement. We'll look at this in more detail later. If you tighten your grip before you play, you'll probably also clench your jaw. Even a tiny amount of activity in these muscles will poke a big stick in the spokes of your wheels of coordination. Check what you're doing with your jaw when getting out of a chair, driving your car or preparing to swing and see if it's not easier when you soften your face.

Of today's golfers, Rory McIlroy demonstrates beautifully the perfect union of strength and great coordination; his technique has been described as 'a motion of effortless fluidity'. Having the strength to perform the action, combined with being able to resist the urge to micro-manage every move, will allow your nervous system to control your muscles far better than you can. The techniques used in the following chapters will help you take your foot off the gas and get a sense of generating power without the effort you feel is necessary.

When it comes to performing complex manoeuvres, it's best to delegate and not coordinate. In other words, do less! Start the ball rolling and then step back and let your body do the rest.

Being On The Ball

Obviously good preparation is key to the success of your shot, but you can undo it all in a moment. Have you ever played a shot before you thought you were ready? You immediately think 'I didn't mean to do that just yet', but it's too late. You get the feeling it wasn't you who just played the shot but some mischievous outside force that had taken over your actions.

This experience is put down to what scientists call *ideomotor movement*, an unconscious or involuntary bodily movement made in response to a thought or an idea rather than to a sensory stimulus. It's also often referred to as 'mischief-making' and has a role in dowsing, playing with a Ouija board and, I believe, in those crucial moments before a putt.

The feeling that the process has just run away from us and taken control out of our hands is because we're thinking too far ahead. By focusing on how we're going to do the activity before we actually need to perform that activity sets everything in place long before the muscles are needed – a bit like revving your engine at the lights.

When you're in the moment, you're in a different state of mind. You're fully aware of every stimulus assailing your senses and tempting you to act, but now you're able to decide *when* and *how* you react.

On the other hand, you can spend ages over the ball and find you've still not moved. When you do finally play it, you could have done better with your eyes shut and one hand tied behind your back. This emphasises the essence of this stimulus-response gap – it's exactly the same regardless of how long you take deciding what you're going to do. It all comes down to what you're thinking at the moment you receive the stimulus to act.

Being in the right frame of mind to use this split second will go a long way to helping you avoid those golfing disasters and become a more consistent player. I know some will say the word disaster is a little strong, but if you fluff that easy putt after three sublime shots to get on the green, it's getting pretty close.

Playing In The Zone [4] – *Poised For Success*

The foundation of a good shot is your stance. If you tighten up going into or while actually in your stance, movement is restricted and your shot is compromised.

This practical exercise will help you to stay poised and keep you in the moment as you prepare to play. You're going to go into your stance by *not* thinking of it as going into your stance, rather being aware of all the actions required.

If at any time you feel the need to tighten your legs or lower back to pull down into your stance, stop and go back a step.

 Try this exercise and see if you can stay in the moment whilst thinking of playing a shot.

51

1) Stand with your driver in your hand.

2) Think of a length of string attached to the top of your head pulling you up so you get taller but check you're not tightening your lower back to do it.

3) Imagine you could switch off your muscles, as if you're going to let yourself collapse, but don't do it, just let the ground under your feet push you up. (More on gravity and your support reflexes later.)

4) Allow for a little movement in your ankles and be aware of your breathing.

5) Visualise a golf ball in the centre of your body just below your navel as if it's suspended in mid air.

6) See the ball going back and up and let it take your torso with it off the top of your legs and let your hips, knees and ankles flex. Be aware of the movement in your ankles and knees.

7) Think of your legs growing out from the centre of your body into the ground and sense the ground pushing gently back. Keep your legs relaxed.

8) Stay in your stance, observe the movement of your ribs and think of one of our 'getting into the moment thoughts', that is, your toes in your socks, the touch of your clothes on your skin, and so on. See full list on page 111.

9) Think about playing the shot and let yourself get right to the point of starting the backswing, but say 'no' – while still thinking the thoughts from the previous step.

10) Finish the practical exercise when you're happy you can stay poised and free in your stance, while thinking of playing the shot without getting set.

The objective is to practise not letting the thought of playing the shot interfere with your poised stance, otherwise you'll be taken out of the moment and your shot will suffer. This will help you recognise inappropriate actions when you come to play the shot later on.

5 The *Now* Moment

Golf is one of those sports where you have time to think before you play. You don't have to react directly to the actions of your opponent, because it's your ball and nobody else is allowed to touch it. You're in total control of your destiny, which also means there's no one else to blame. However, sometimes having the luxury of time to think about how you're going to play can be a huge disadvantage.

In the final moment just before the club makes contact with the ball, do you sometimes hear a little voice inside groaning '*Oh no*', or worse? How about when you throw a screwed-up piece of paper towards the wastebasket or make the decision to overtake on a winding road? It doesn't matter if you know it's not going to work just before you act, it appears too late to change. All you can do is watch helplessly as you fulfil the prophecy like a runaway train hurtling towards the buffers. It's as if part of us can see into the future, yet we don't have the ability to alter our decision in the present. It's a pretty cruel trick when you think about it – especially when that voice brags that it '*told you so*' when it does go wrong. It's not much consolation when you've just realised your gentle tap was anything but.

However, all is not lost. I believe this temporary time-shift experience or 'future echo' could be the gap between the planning and execution processes, as discovered by Haggard and Eimer – the one that occurs with all actions. It's just particularly noticeable when you're taking your time over an action such as a putt. With practice, it's possible to step into this moment and take control of the runaway train to execute your intended stroke with far greater accuracy.

In my view, this is the difference between being *in* or *out* of The Zone. When we're in The Zone, we have the feeling of being in control. In place of being the harbinger of doom, that little voice becomes an expert calmly examining all the variables, and it rapidly presents us with the solution.

What's On Your Mind?

Have a go at the questions below. I ask these of all the golfers I work with, and it's amazing how many don't have an answer – or at least have to think about them for some time to come up with one. These relate to that vital moment before you play:

1) **What *exactly* do you think about before and during a shot? Do you talk to yourself? Do you have a mental checklist or use imagery?**

2) **What determines when you start to play your shot? Do you say 'now' or have a particular word, cue or a set of criteria that has to be met before you play?**

3) **Is there a moment just before you play your shot where you realise it's going to be a good or bad one?**

4) **If you answered yes to question 3, are you able to stop or change your shot if you know it's not good?**

Don't worry if you didn't have an answer for each one. It's the same for most sports people, including a number of Olympic athletes I've interviewed. I believe it's because we're not in the moment and consequently not fully aware of what we're thinking.

Obviously you're aware that you're playing a shot, but whether you're aware of what's *actually* going through your mind and what's happening with your body is another matter.

This is the crux of the whole performance thing. What you're thinking at the very moment you decide to 'go for it' has a much bigger influence on the outcome of your action than your previous preparation. It's pretty obvious really, isn't it? You can fluff the most carefully thought-out shot in a moment if your thinking is wrong at the time of the shot. Get this bit wrong, and you won't be able to execute your plan with the accuracy you'd have liked.

So, here you are standing over the ball waiting to play the shot you have in mind. You're in a sort of limbo just before the 'now moment'. This is where you hover between thinking and doing. Your thoughts are constantly sending signals to your muscles. In fact, every pathway from your brain eventually finds its way to a muscle. At some point the flow of electrical activity reaches a threshold, and the gates open for the extra pulse to kick the muscles into action. Any doubts at this time will delay this moment and add more signals – invariably conflicting ones – to the process.

This is the moment where you have the greatest influence over whether you succeed or fail, so it's pretty important really. Before it, you still have options open to you. After it, everything has kicked off, and you can't recall your actions or change the result. Skill is about minimising the errors in translation, so you can execute physically something pretty close to what you had in mind.

When athletes talk about being in The Zone, I believe they're fully conscious of, and have absolute clarity about, the processes that occur in this moment. Therefore, they experience a heightened sense of awareness and, as a consequence, a greater degree of control over their actions. The paradox is that it doesn't feel like control in the usual sense. In fact, it feels incredibly easy. When it comes to your own game, you'll wonder why it can't be like that all the time!

It's Golf Jim, But Not As We Know It!

When you're about to tee off, the actions you perform are based on your perception of what's required to carry out the shot. According to Haggard and Eimer's research, your brain will have constructed a plan, worked out what it's going to feel like, tried very hard to execute that plan and will then have told you what just happened. You won't contemplate taking the shot until all of the familiar sensations you associate with your swing are in place. For instance, you might feel the urge to:

- **Tense your lower back**

- **Lift your shoulders**

- **Tighten your grip**

- **Clench your jaw**

- **Hold your breath**

or do all of them!

You'll probably have a number of such errors present in your technique but, because they're an integral part of your preparation, you won't notice them. In order to eradicate these habitual faults, you need to blow away all the froth that you've built up over the years so you can fully appreciate what you're doing. And guess what? This can be done very effectively by getting 'into the moment'.

Earlier, we touched the end of our noses to get a sense of what being in the moment entails. Now we'll do something a little more challenging, but apply the same principle. I'd like you to perform a swing 'in the moment'.

Playing In The Zone [5] – *The Now Moment*

Note: I've avoided using golfing terminology in the following instructions. I'd like you to focus on your movements in a non-golfing way. If you start to think about this as a swing, you'll put your golf hat on in a second and resort to your usual habits and get nothing from it. The objective here is to get into the moment with a club in your hands while *not* thinking of playing a shot. This way, you can prevent your usual preparations from taking over and, instead, observe every action you're actually doing (or feel you need to do) and determine whether it's contributing to your technique or impeding it.

Don't be concerned about getting this right or wrong. You need to remain detached from the thought of performing it correctly and stay non-judgemental about the outcome.

 You can do this first as a practice swing at home before taking it to the range and course.

1) **Stand with your driver and use the techniques from the Playing in The Zone [3] and [4] exercises to get into your stance.**

2) **Be aware of every part of your hands making contact with the club handle and get a sense of using your forearm muscles connected to your elbows working the hands to lightly grip the club.**

3) Check that your eyes are not fixed and that your face, jaw, shoulders, legs and back are relaxed – and that you're still breathing.

4) Think of raising your club, but instead say '*no*' while going back through the step above.

5) Notice what you want to do to start, and ask yourself whether it's really necessary.

6) When you're satisfied all is still, say '*now*' (in your head) and start your backswing and let the club do the work. If '*now*' doesn't do it for you, try other words such as '*yes*', '*go*', '*damn the torpedoes*' or whatever works best.

Repeat this as often as you can, but approach it as if it's the first time every time you do it. This way you'll prevent your preparation becoming a habit and avoid the dangers of slipping into your familiar routine. It's a challenge to approach something you do many times a day with a beginner's mind, but it helps if you rotate the 'getting into the moment thoughts' (see page 111) and pick up on something pertinent to the moment such as the weather and sounds. Also try *The Performing Artist* on page 87, as this will also help you to 'keep it new'.

The next step is to take this onto the driving range, but don't let the addition of the ball change anything. On your first visit use as little effort as possible and don't be concerned about how far the ball goes. The objective is to get a sense of how you can make the club work for you.

On following visits start to experiment with adding a little more effort. If done correctly you'll find the best distances are achieved with timing and free-flowing movement – with little perception of effort. Accept you may have to undo some of your existing technique, and take a step or two back to experiment with doing something different.

Just Say No

When you perform a task you've done thousands of times before, you can practically switch off and become oblivious to much of what you're doing. Many parts of that task are taken for granted and done without conscious thought, allowing your habitual way of doing them to take over. If you're not knowingly controlling any one part of your technique, there'll be more room for errors to creep in.

Placing your attention on every detail is a way of getting into the moment and, with practice, requires very little effort on your part. Once you combine your technical knowledge with the ability to execute it with minimal error, you're well on the way to becoming a more consistent and contented golfer. This can only be done when you're fully conscious of what's *really* happening when you play. Libet, the man whose research challenged our concept of free will, came with up a gem of an alternative: 'free won't'. That is, although we may have unconscious activity firing away and tempting us into action, we can still say *no* to the urge and give ourselves time to stop and think before we act.

As you stand over the ball about to play your shot, you have three options:

1) **Play it the usual way using your habitual patterns.**

2) **Play it differently – allowing it to feel wrong.**

3) **Do nothing.**

Number three may not sound like an option at all, as you could hardly stand there all day doing nothing, but it's still useful for our purposes. If you take your shot without stopping to think through the steps that will keep you in the moment, you'll rely on your usual habits. Right up to the very last moment, you can still say 'no', do nothing and keep your options open, while checking you're not getting set to play by tightening up or holding your breath. If you start to notice you're doing something to prepare in your old way, you can still stop and go back to square one.

At some point in your preparation you'll want to do something that feels right, such as lifting the shoulders or tightening your grip. This is where you have to keep saying to yourself that you don't need to do it – it's your old habit pleading with you to just get on with it! You've got to resist this urge, stay in the moment, say 'no' and not let yourself be coaxed down that familiar path.

Golfers need to be particularly wary of repeating the same movement in the same controlled manner over and over again, as it can have a detrimental effect on more than just your muscles.

The Y-Word

Possibly one of the worst nightmares for any golfer is to experience the misery of the so-called Yips. Sufferers use terms such as jerking, stabbing, jabbing and twitching to describe an abrupt, involuntary movement in the wrist of their dominant hand. In the worst cases, researchers believe the cause is focal dystonia, whereas many players may have symptoms of the Yips but not have a specific neurological condition. Mature golfers with a low handicap and 25 or more years under their belt are particularly susceptible to this dreaded condition. Studies into the Yips by Smith (2000) and Adler (2004) concluded that age, excessive use of the muscles involved, the complexity of the technique – plus intense concentration – make it worse. Is some of this starting to sound familiar?

In a play-off between prevention and cure, prevention wins every time. It's far better to avoid the Yips than to wait for it to happen and then attempt to cure it. Playing more often in the relaxed, effortless state of The Zone, the opposite of the contributory conditions suggested by the research, will help you to avoid this dreaded curse.

But why do some golfers experience it while others don't?

It's the same reason as why some computer users get repetitive strain injuries (RSI), eyestrain or back pain while others don't. It's not what you do it's the way that you do it. Obviously you can't avoid getting older, but you do have control over how you use your muscles, how you execute your technique and how you concentrate. Control over how you concentrate? Check whether you furrow your brow, tighten your jaw or stiffen your neck when you need to concentrate. All these will have an effect on your coordination and lead to excessive use of your muscles. You don't need to do anything physical to concentrate, but many of us do!

If you're already plagued by the Yips, or something similar, it's pointless trying to prevent the intrusive jerk at the time of taking your shot. It's already sitting in the wings waiting for its cue as soon as you think about the putt. The involuntary muscle contraction has become an integral part of a conditioned reflex of your putting habit. The set of muscle actions required for your putt are effectively hard-wired into your brain.

Now remember your brain is eager to reproduce those familiar and comfortable patterns to carry out your wishes, including the offending *Yip*, whether you want it or not! You can prevent using your flawed pattern and contain it by implementing the techniques in this book. Staying in the moment, focusing on the intermediate stages and saying '*no*' at the point of execution, gives you the opportunity to do something different. In other words, use an alternative set of patterns to perform your putt, and not the one containing the Y*ip*.

In the next chapter we'll look at other long-term implications for your 'body mechanics' of playing *and* living out of the moment and how you can improve them. Before we do, let's return to see how Tom is getting on.

Tom's Predicament — Part Two

 Tom's problem of holding excessive tension in his neck and shoulders may have started due to playing under stress, but the solution doesn't lie in learning to relax. Stress is no longer the cause, and therefore stress-relieving techniques are not part of the solution.

Playing with his shoulders tense for so long has changed his concept of what's involved in preparing for his shot. Therefore, it's his concept that he needs to address before he makes any other changes to his technique.

The moment he starts to think about his swing, he sets himself up in his habitual way. He is focusing on an action that has yet to happen, that is, the club head making contact with the ball. Therefore, he *cannot be in the moment*. You may think that, like any good golfer, he'll be checking his stance and running through his pre-shot preparations, but while he has the thought of the swing in his mind, the muscles that will do it for him are ready and active – and thus interfering with his stance. In Tom's case we know this involves tightening his neck and lifting his shoulders slightly.

He should be absorbed in the act of his stance, so he'll be poised before he starts the backswing. This way he'll instantly recognise the tension and be able to stop and start over again.

So, how does Tom change his technique? He knows something is wrong but has not as yet discovered the real cause? He has an idea that it's something he started to do prior to the shot, because he had previously been able to play it with relatively few difficulties.

His coach has highlighted the tension build up in his neck and shoulders, yet he lacks the self-awareness and observational skills to determine what's causing this. Besides, he cannot feel this for himself because it's a habit and part of his technique. He's unable to prevent it, because he can't stop doing something he doesn't know he's doing! As soon as he thinks about playing, he applies this tension and won't start the swing until it's present. It may not be much, but it's enough to significantly alter the dynamics of his swing.

Okay, by now you'll know the answer: he has to be in the moment to prevent any unnecessary action in his preparation and he has to not do what feels right – because that's his usual habit. But it's one thing for him to understand this on a theoretical level – or when applying it to a non-golfing act he cares little about – but what about on the tee at the start of a vital hole? It will be more of a challenge, because the last thing he'll want to do in this situation is something that feels wrong!

However, it's not just a matter of getting into the moment to take greater control over his preparation. After years of using his body with these inefficient actions, his natural, reflexive coordination has all but disappeared. In addition to focusing on the moment and 'what' he's doing, he also needs to pay attention to 'how' he's going about it. Luckily for Tom, and for us, this makes getting into the moment easier and even more rewarding.

6 A Moving Experience

Living at an ever-increasing pace in today's demanding world has had an impact on our behaviour to the point where scientists now refer to it as the 'rushing disease'. There always seems to be a deadline and, as we find more ingenious ways to communicate, it gets harder to get away from it all. Perhaps the only time many of us have a chance of being truly in the moment is when we're playing our sport. But being in the moment doesn't necessarily mean you're going to perform at your peak. There's another factor.

Imagine what it would be like trying to drive your car if, when you steer to the right, your car goes left? Of course, it would be immediately obvious there was a fault because you can see it for yourself. You could, with practice, learn how to cope with this fault and adjust your driving accordingly, but it would be better to fix the fault. What if every time you get into your stance you tightened your lower back? You won't notice it. You'll have associated the 'feel' of your lower back with your stance. So when you think everything is as it should be you may actually be holding excessive tension in your body.

You may, without knowing it, be using your body in a way that leads to poor movement and control. This makes complex movements and techniques harder to execute than they should be. I'm sure you're well aware of what constitutes a good swing on a theoretical level. You know exactly what needs to be done but somehow you just can't do it in a way you would like to.

When it comes down to putting the theory into practice, you may be misinterpreting your own instructions. It's a sort of Chinese Whispers: what comes out at the end is very different from what you *thought* you put in at the start. However, if you've learned bad habits relating to movement, it's possible to unlearn them. A better understanding of how your body is put together and how it can move will help to significantly reduce the unnecessary bits and pieces we unknowingly bring to our technique. If we drove our cars half as badly as most of us *drive* our bodies, they would constantly breakdown. The human body is remarkably resilient but still has limits.

Biomechanics And Spanners

I believe living *out* of the moment can lead to faulty movement patterns. Rushing about performing our daily activities with our minds three steps ahead can drastically reduce our self-awareness. For example, the next time you go to lift your golf bag, see whether you're tensing in anticipation of picking it up – even before you've taken hold of the strap. This tension is not necessary, and getting set to lift the bag prematurely will reduce the efficiency of your actions as you move towards it.

Every player knows the importance of being relaxed but do you know what a relaxed state feels like? If the tension in your muscles has been gradually building over the years due to inefficient movement, the threshold for feeling relaxed raises with it. What passes for relaxed today may have felt as tight as a drum ten years ago.

We can sit all day at a computer with our shoulders held up around our ears and be so distracted by *what* we're doing that we give no thought to *how* we're doing it. We don't realise we're sitting with this tension until the muscles start to ache. The same applies to driving in rush hour traffic. And what do we do when we get home? We collapse into the armchair and spend the evening slumping. We go from one extreme to the other without spending any time in the middle. When you get out onto the golf course, do you suddenly get a new body?

From my own experience and from working closely with well over a thousand people from all sports and walks of life during the last twelve years, I believe the majority of adults move in a less-than-efficient way. As a consequence, they perform below their true potential, suffer injury and develop poor posture. Okay, this does sound a little dramatic but, until I was shown otherwise, I was oblivious to my own shortcomings in relation to movement. I suffered the injuries but didn't recognise the cause.

If our coordination is below par, muscles will be pulling when they should be letting go and, as a consequence, will be acting against the muscles that are performing the movement. It's a bit like trying to drive your car with the brake on. Doing something thousands and thousands of times doesn't guarantee perfection. As the coach said, *'Practice makes permanent, not necessarily perfect!'*

Eyesight can slowly deteriorate without us noticing – until we have a test and suddenly everything looks crystal clear again. The same is true of our movement. The difficulty here is that we cannot go and try on a top golfer's body to get a sense of what a good swing should feel like. However, what we can do is go back to the basics, unlearn the bad habits and give the body a fighting chance to achieve what we really want it to do.

Don't Panic

I'm not going to tell you yet again about the importance of getting the golf basics right, as I'm sure you've heard this enough already. We're going to look at something even more fundamental than your golf basics, something that is key to playing good golf or, indeed, any sport. We're going to look at the basics that underpin how you go about getting your grip, stance, swing and any other movement.

Every movement you make consists of a chain of actions that set you up for the next action in the link. As a golfer, you'll be aware of the effect of getting one link in the chain wrong. If your stance is poor, your swing will suffer. Undue tension in your body as you raise the club will affect the trajectory of the club, and that in turn is going to mean the club head isn't going to make the right contact with the ball.

The following section contains a number of simple experiments. I call them *Body Basics*, and they're designed to help you improve your concept of your body and consequently how you use it.

Getting To Know *You*

These procedures are adapted from those I use when teaching The Alexander Technique. I'll ask you to be in the moment and focused, so you can observe how you move and act. This will help increase self-awareness.

Let's start at the top and work our way down:

Body Basics [1] – *Head And Neck*

Do you know where your head sits on your spine? You've probably never been asked this question before, but where you think this point is could have a huge impact on your performance. Have a go. Point to where you think this is before continuing to the next page.

No peeking!

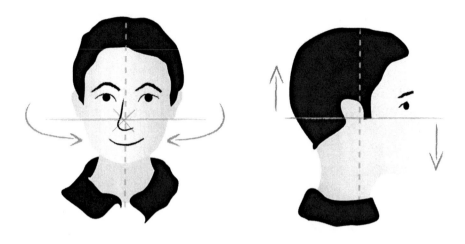

Fig 6.1 The atlanto-occipital joint (where your head sits on your spine) is much higher up than most people think.

If you ask one hundred people to point to where their head sits on their spine at least ninety-five will point to somewhere on the back of and half way down their neck. The actual joint, known as the atlanto-occipital joint, is higher than most people appreciate and is located towards the centre of the skull. Try it. Ask your friends this question and see where they think it is.

So why does it matter? How will it help your golf?

The muscles attached at the base of your skull are connected at the other end to the top vertebrae, and these are the most sensitive muscles, by some distance, in your body. These tiny muscles help coordinate muscle activity in conjunction with other senses. It matters to your golf because, if these highly sensitive muscles spanning this joint aren't active due to tension in the outer layer of muscles, they're unable to feed vital information about your movement and orientation to your nervous system. If your guess at its position was someway off the true location, it's probably because you're not letting your head move from this point. You could be preventing your reflexes from coordinating your movement.

In addition to reflexes, the weight of your head sitting in the wrong place will place undue stresses on the rest of your body.

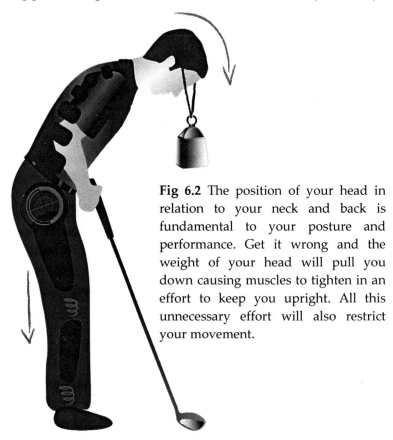

Fig 6.2 The position of your head in relation to your neck and back is fundamental to your posture and performance. Get it wrong and the weight of your head will pull you down causing muscles to tighten in an effort to keep you upright. All this unnecessary effort will also restrict your movement.

Your head weighs around 4.5 kilograms (10 lbs). That's a heavy load to be carried in the wrong place. I believe the biggest single thing you can do to improve your performance from a biomechanical point of view is to learn how to allow your head to balance and articulate from the anatomically correct place on top of your spine.

When you allow your head to release forward from this joint when you're going into your stance, your spine stretches out and relaxes the whole of your body while maintaining length up the front of your torso. This happens without any need to hold the posture, because the release of the neck removes the muscle activity that would otherwise pull your spine out of its natural, neutral shape.

Getting A Head Start

'Keep your head still' or 'keep your head over the ball' is advice given to every beginner, but the strange thing is that the top players don't keep their heads still. A study by Sanders and Owens in 1992 found that experts move their heads more during the swing than novices. However, the experts do stabilise head movement just before and after contact with the ball. Scientists believe the reason why top golfers can hit the ball further with less apparent effort may be due to the movement of the head at the right time.

It may be that, as a beginner, keeping your head still does make it easier to learn the technique initially. However, if you continue to follow this advice, you could be doing so by tightening your neck, fixing your head on the spine and thus restricting the range of movement in your upper body – and even down to your hips. Imagine how difficult it would be to swing wearing a jacket that's two sizes too small. If you stiffen your neck, even by only a fraction, to keep your head still, you're limiting your rotation and harming your chances of ever wearing the green one!

Finding the right rhythm to generate speed to the clubhead requires a coordinated sequence of movements from different parts of your body with crucial timing, especially the upper body and hips. Free movement can only occur if your balance is good and you can maintain your stance with minimal muscle activity. Try a few practice swings after checking first that your jaw is relaxed, and let this release flow through your body. Stay aware of your breathing and see that it doesn't suddenly force itself out as you swing. Staying aware of your breathing can help to release the brake and free up your rotation.

 Let's get your head moving from the correct location.

1) **Place both your index fingers in the groove behind your ears. The joint from which your head moves is roughly in between your two fingers and almost level with your eyes; it's the point where the two lines cross in Fig 6.1.**

2) **Remove your fingers and move your head to the left and right from that point without the shoulders moving.**

3) **Now look up and down allowing you head to move on the pivot point like a seesaw.**

Whether sitting reading a book or looking down at the ball, let your head move from this point and prevent your neck from dropping forward. In the next chapter we'll put this into practice while assuming your stance.

Body Basics [2] – *Eyes*

Vision plays a fundamental role in balance and coordination. For a quick demonstration compare the difference between standing on one leg with your eyes open and then with your eyes shut. What you see is combined with signals from your inner ear, joints and muscles to make sense of the outside world. Travel sickness is a result of a mismatch between your visual and balance senses sending conflicting information to a confused brain.

Probably one of the first tips you were given in golf was to keep your eyes on the ball for the swing. This is to ensure your head stays in the same place, so the club head returns to address as you swing through the ball. However, many people have a general habit of fixing their eyes on an object – something that they look at for a certain length of time, such as a TV or computer screen. The next time you're looking for your car keys, check you're not using your eyes like search beams! When you're looking at the ball, you don't need to 'send anything to it'. Light bounces off the ball and comes *in* to the eyeball – not the other way around.

If you fix your eyes and stare at your golf ball, you're also likely to tighten your neck muscles. As we've just seen in the previous Body Basic, a stiff neck reduces the efficiency of your swing, and all movement for that matter. If you can 'relax' your eyes, your neck will be freer and allow for better movement.

 Try this quick exercise for your eyes.

1) **Hold your index finger about arms length in front of your nose.**

2) **Relax your jaw and let the image of your finger arrive at your eyes.**

3) **Now move your head around, from the right place, but keep your eyes on your finger.**

4) **Sense your eyes moving in your skull.**

When you're shaping up for your swing, rather than thinking 'keep your eyes on the ball' turn it around to thinking 'keep the ball in your eyes'. Remember, the light comes into your eyes after bouncing off the ball, so you don't have to stare and fix your eyes on it. If your eyes are open, the image comes to you without any effort on your part.

Avoid thinking of the image in front of you as a ball because you may start to worry about hitting it. If you've set up correctly and you keep the image of it in your sight, the club will hit the ball as you swing through. Soften your jaw and remember your eyes don't project anything to the ball. When you start the backswing, don't use your neck or head to fix the eyes on the ball but let your neck and eyes stay free – and the muscles behind your eyes will do the rest.

Body Basics [3] – *Shoulders*

We've talked about excessive tension in the shoulders and we saw in Tom's case how it can become a hidden habit. It's actually a very common habit and can be seen whenever people lift an object, grip something or use a keyboard or steering wheel. From our point of view it has to be eliminated right at the start of the preparation and monitored throughout the stroke.

The shoulder joint is a ball and socket and located not surprisingly at the top of the arm, yet many people move as if it's situated halfway between the neck and arm.

 This simple exercise can help you to relax your shoulders.

1) Stand facing a wall just inside your arms length so you can easily reach it; let your arms rest by your sides.

2) If you have a partner handy, ask them to stand behind you and place their hands lightly on your shoulders.

3) Start with your non-dominant side and imagine your arm is getting longer with the thumb pointing toward the floor.

4) Keep this thought as you bring it out slightly, then up in front of you to let your hand rest lightly on the wall opposite your shoulder.

5) As you move your arm, think of the location of the ball and socket joint and allow your arm to move from this point without lifting your shoulder. The contact of your partner's hands will feedback whether you have raised your shoulder.

6) If you find your shoulder is lifting, you can think of softening your jaw a little; just be aware of the gap between the upper and lower teeth and see if this helps.

7) Repeat this with your dominant arm and then try moving both at the same time with just a thought of them releasing out from your back just before you move them.

We'll come back to this movement in the next chapter when placing your hands on the club.

Body Basics [4] – *Backs*

How do you know when you're getting old? When your back goes out more often than you do! Apologies if you've heard this before, but it makes a good point and it's no laughing matter really – especially if it stops you playing.

Back pain is an all-too-common problem, and not just for the older player. Our stone-age body doesn't seem to be suited to the modern world, and hours spent inactive at desks or in cars takes its toll – and our backs take most of the punishment.

So surely a round of golf is the ideal antidote? Certainly, but putting on your golf clothes and getting out onto the course doesn't suddenly get you a new body. The hours spent sitting about, or more likely slumping, will condition your body and muscles just as effectively as a few hours at the gym, only not in a way you'd like. To then ask the same body to cope with the twists, strains and forces of a swing is to tempt fate. So what you do away from the course can influence your game more than you think.

Golf can put tremendous stress on the back. However, with good coordination and technique, this can be greatly reduced. One of the best things you can do for your back is to know the location of your hip joints. This will allow you to bend from the right place and free up the muscles of the lower back, so they don't interfere unnecessarily with your swing.

Most of us bend from the lower back. In fact, it's easier on your back and better for your performance to move with the pelvis and back together. Watch an adult bend to pick something up off the floor, and then compare it with a young child. You'll see quite a difference.

To find your hip joints, use your fingers to trace the bony parts at the front of the pelvis above each leg. If you're wearing trousers the points are generally at the opening of the front pockets. Now walk the fingers down toward the legs and press in until they sink in a little.

These are your hip joints and this is where you should move from when getting into your stance. The back should not round at all.

 This chair exercise will help you to appreciate where you can bend to reduce stress on your back.

1) Sit on a chair and tilt forward. Do you collapse at the front or round your back?

2) Now imagine that you can hinge where you make contact with the chair and perform the movement again, letting your spine and pelvis move together – see Fig 6.3 over the page.

3) Tilt forward without rounding your back and hold this position for a few moments. Now let go and your torso will tilt back to the upright position without effort.

We'll return to this movement later to see how it can improve your stance.

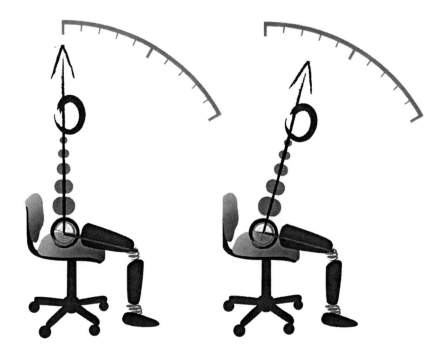

Fig 6.3 Moving from your hip joints will keep your pelvis and back together and reduce stress on your lower back

Body Basics [5] – *Legs*

You've probably been told before to think of your legs as springs when in your stance. This is vitally important, as it allows your body to stay poised and free of inappropriate tension. This allows you to generate the power needed to swing your club or apply the deft touch for putting.

However, as mentioned earlier, you can't suddenly change your muscle tone and coordination just by simply picking up your club. How you move in your daily activities will have a huge influence on how you 'use' yourself on the course. Regaining poise away from your golf can greatly improve your technique.

 I call this one pendulums – the reason will become obvious in a moment.

1) First, locate your hips joints while standing – see previous section.

2) Keep your fingers on your hip joints as you walk on the spot and let your legs release from this point without your pelvis moving.

3) Now walk forward by letting go from your hip joints, and appreciate that the ground is pushing back up in response to your feet as they land.

4) Let your knee bend to lift your foot off the ground and let the lower leg swing through effortlessly like a pendulum. (See Fig 6.4 on the next page.)

5) Imagine you're stroking the ground away from under your feet to get a gentle push up and forward.

Walking provides an ideal activity in which to experience effortless movement while releasing tension from the shoulders and lower back. It can also help to remind you of the location of your hips joints. That, in turn, will improve your stance.

Whether you're walking to and from your car or up to your golf ball, you can use the walk to focus and get into the moment. You can learn how to use an effortless walk between shots to loosen up your muscles – especially if you're under a bit of stress.

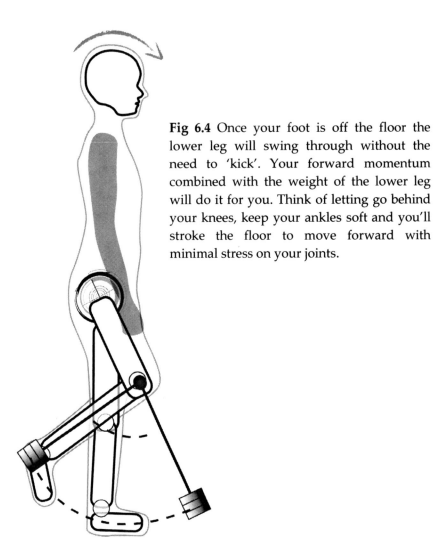

Fig 6.4 Once your foot is off the floor the lower leg will swing through without the need to 'kick'. Your forward momentum combined with the weight of the lower leg will do it for you. Think of letting go behind your knees, keep your ankles soft and you'll stroke the floor to move forward with minimal stress on your joints.

Body Basics [6] – **Balance Reflexes**

Even before birth our brain knows the difference between up and down. The fluid in our inner ear acts like a spirit level and works with our developing head-righting and neck reflexes to aid balance and coordination. It's quite an amazing mechanism capable of directing every muscle in the body to switch on and switch off at exactly the right time, so we can achieve feats as complicated as the golf swing.

Well, that's the theory. I'm sure you've already discovered for yourself that this isn't always the case. Newton's third law of gravity states that the mutual actions of two bodies upon each other are always equal and in opposite directions. This is more commonly known as, "For every action there is an equal opposite reaction". So, in response to the downward pull exerted by gravity, there's an upward push from every contact point, known as the ground reaction force. This helps to stabilise your stance.

 This technique will help you to promote poise – a vital component of your performance.

1) **Stand with your feet about hip width apart.**

2) **Place your attention on a point about four centimetres below your navel and in the centre of your body. Visualise a golf ball with light flowing out from it through your legs to the floor, up your spine, along your arms and through the top of your head. (See Fig 6.5.)**

3) **Imagine that your legs can grow out from this point towards the floor and, as they do, you get a push**

coming back through the spine and out through the top of your head.

4) Release your muscles a little and get a sense of your bones balancing on top of each other without letting yourself lose height.

5) Relax your ankles and allow for a little movement.

6) Relax your feet and allow your toes to spread a little.

7) Try this before you get into your stance and allow the ground to support you, so you can release excessive tension from your body.

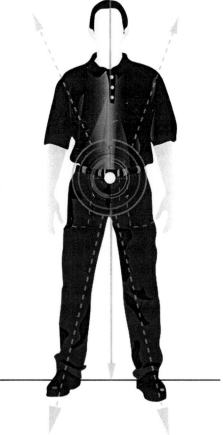

Fig 6.5 To stand tall requires less effort than to slump or to hold the military style 'stand to attention'. Poise means using appropriate effort for the task in hand. Standing requires far less effort than most people habitually use.

So whether you're running, jumping, standing, sitting or swinging, there's a push coming back from the floor to help balance and coordinate your movement. I've found an appreciation of this 'push' reduces undue tension, promotes poise and frees up movement – so take Obi wan Kenobe's advice and learn to 'use the force'!

Undue tension in your body can 'override' your built-in postural reflexes and get in the way of your body's balance mechanisms. It means that, instead of letting the ground 'push' you up, you start pulling yourself down into it. In this state it requires more effort, as your muscles struggle to keep the body upright.

Celebrate The Mundane

These Body Basics can be done on their own or as part of your everyday activities. You now have something to do when you find yourself standing in a queue or waiting for the slow-coaches in front of you on the course. You need never be agitated or bored again.

Performing your usual mundane daily tasks with some awareness of how you're moving gives you the perfect opportunity to practise being in the moment. It also helps improve your 'body mechanics' by reducing poor movement patterns. If you find yourself pushing the trolley around a supermarket with a sense of lightness in your body while reaching for the frozen peas in the freezer, and it's actually enjoyable. You're in the moment and using your body as nature intended.

On the other hand, if you can't wait to get out of there and back onto the golf course, you'll be rushing around, misusing your body and not setting yourself up for a good back nine. Take a tight body onto the course and you'll put yourself at a greater risk of injury. You'll probably need that bag of peas for your knees when you get home.

Live in the moment as often as you can. What you do away from the course, no matter how mundane, will help you no end when you get back on it.

Tom's Predicament — Part Three

 Tom had unknowingly learned to lift his shoulders every time he prepared to swing, until eventually it became an integral part of his technique. He has long since lost his sense of 'natural' activity because his basics, or movement building blocks, contain unnecessary actions.

So, although he can now focus and get into the moment, he still needs to change how he's using his body, otherwise all efforts to solve the problem are starting too far down the line *after* his habitual preparations have kicked in.

The habits associated with his golf are deeply entrenched; even the sight of a club will trigger his habitual response. Before he can successfully correct his technique, he'll need to work on himself – away from golf – using the procedures in the section above. Once he has a grasp of these basics and is able to apply them in his everyday activities, his movement and coordination will improve, followed quickly by changes in his muscles that will help him rebuild the foundation for all his actions.

He's now ready to step up a gear and practise getting into the moment for playing in The Zone when he's out on the course.

Playing In The Zone [6] – *The Performing Artist*

Trying to prevent your usual habitual response when performing an act you've done thousands of times before can be a challenge. As with Tom, just the sight and feel of a club will trigger hard-wired responses in your own brain. Those fast, automatic reactions can take you out of the moment and lead you down a path containing any number of unnecessary actions that you've accumulated over the years – and they could be cramping your style. The best way to change the output and allow for something new to happen is to change the input.

 Have a go at the following and try to take it seriously.

1) Take a club out of your bag and place it in front of you on a table.

2) Focus on the movement of your ribs and release your jaw a fraction to soften your face.

3) Be conscious of moving your eyes as you look at the object in front of you and see the different colours, textures, shadows, lines and patterns. See it with an artist's eye for detail.

4) Avoid labelling each part as you see it. How would you describe it to someone without using any golf terms?

5) Now reach forward to pick it up and sense what your fingers are making contact with.

6) Wrap your hands around the handle – but don't think of it as a handle or attempt to get your grip right.

7) **Pick it up and feel its weight and still maintain awareness of your face and breathing.**

8) **When you next take a club from your bag on the course, have a brief think about what you've just experienced.**

9) **You're now ready to hug a tree.**

Yes, it may seem a bit wacky, but the objective is to keep your mind alert, open and focused on the present. Once you see the object as a golf club, you've labelled it and accessed your 'golf brain' and compartmentalised the instrument in front of you as a putter or driver. Anything you now do with the club is now firmly connected to your habits and feelings associated with that particular club.

You can try this looking at or handling any object. When you're on the course, try looking at the trees, grass, bunkers and flags and put yourself into your 'first day at school' mode; look for something 'new' you haven't noticed before. When you're in the moment, more outcomes are possible, including that peach of a shot that usually eludes you.

7 Seven Experiments To Transform Your Golf

It's always seven isn't it! Seven reasons why you should buy this or that or seven steps to happiness, instant success or world domination. Not sure why, but seven does seem to be the magic number, so we'll stick with it here.

I prefer to use the term experiments and not exercises, because I'd like you to do these with the detached, objective mind of a scientist observing cause and effect. In other words, observe what you're thinking at the time of the movement and what result that brings about. The experiments are not intended for repetitive use, as with an exercise. In fact, you may only need to do some of these once to get the idea.

What you learn from each experiment can be directly applied to your golf and to everyday activities. You can also use them to practise the art of focusing and bringing yourself into a state of stillness, where you become acutely aware of every movement you make and can determine whether it's helping or impeding an activity.

With all these experiments, check you're *not* 'concentrating' by making a face or holding your breath. In fact, it's best you don't try to concentrate at all. Just be slightly curious and vaguely interested in the results, and this will help you get into the right frame of mind. Use as little effort as possible for the movements, and let your body flow.

Let's get started. It'll be easier if you can get someone to read to you or, alternatively, there are audio instructions available on the website. (See Useful Resources on page 153.)

1. The Full Back

This is an easy and effective way to recognise and release undue stress from your body after a long day on the course or at the office. The purpose of the books under your head (see Fig 7.1) is to keep the spine in its natural alignment so your head doesn't tip back and pull your neck down. To determine the height of the books, stand with your shoulder blades touching a wall and with your head sitting on top of your spine, as in Body Basics 1. Get someone to measure the gap between the base of the skull and the wall. This is the depth of books you'll require.

 Your body will thank you for taking time out to do this.

1) Lie on your back on the floor with your head supported by a few books and your knees up and feet flat on the floor. Rest your hands on your torso just below your ribs.

2) Be aware of the floor and of where you're making contact with it – the back of your head, shoulder blades, elbows, pelvis and the feet. (Specifically think of letting the heels drop while keeping the toes in contact with the floor.) Allow yourself to be supported by the floor.

3) Notice the space between your torso and arms and allow your ribs to move into this area as you breathe. You don't need to take deep breaths. Instead, just let the incoming air inflate your lungs and move your ribs. Let the movement of your ribs move your hands.

4) Be aware of yourself lying on the floor and just let the air flow in and out of your nose. In this horizontal position the weight of your skull is no longer resting on your spine, so the intervertebral discs will start to thicken and your spine will lengthen.

5) Check that you're not holding any tension in your body and allow the floor to support you. By releasing the habitual patterns in this position, gravity will re-align your body and remove the twists the day has put there.

6) Think of releasing out from your centre so your arms and legs can 'grow' and your back can lengthen and widen.

7) Spend about twenty minutes in this position while sensing the movement of your ribs – and relax.

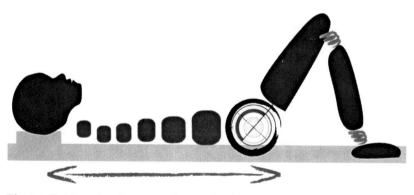

Fig 7.1 Taking the day out of your body. Let gravity put your bones where they're supposed to be rather than where your muscles pull them. Taking the weight off your spine will allow your discs to thicken and push your head and pelvis away from each other.

2. Face Value

You're probably familiar with the term 'poker face'. Players learn how to control reactions such as raising the eyebrows or movements of the mouth, as even the slightest twitch could reveal the quality of their hand. Obviously you don't need to worry about quite such minor details for your game, but what you do with your face can still affect your shot.

Our facial muscles are very sensitive to what we think – it's an important part of communication. However, our expressions not only inform others what we're thinking, but they also feedback into our own emotions.

People say 'smile and the world looks a better place' – and even if it's a false smile it can still work. Hopefully you'll be enjoying your round of golf so much that you'll be smiling all the time and get a lift from it, but if it's not going well what are you doing with your face? Does the effort of trying harder to concentrate do something to your face? For most people, this involves at least one of the following

- **Furrowing our brow**

- **Fixing our eyes (staring)**

- **Tightening our jaw**

- **Pursing our lips**

- **And holding our breath for good measure**

All of these actions can actually interfere with your ability to focus and even interfere with your movement. Tension in the face and jaw muscles will tighten your neck muscles and consequently your shoulders and back. At the same time, fixing your eyes can upset your balance and coordination. It's possible to focus without pulling a face but, as with many other reactions, it's become a habit to make a face – otherwise we don't feel it's possible to concentrate.

Have a go at this. Then apply this same technique next time you're preparing to take a long putt and you feel you need to do something with your face to make it work.

 This simple technique can have a surprisingly big affect on your game.

1) **Allow your teeth to part a little but leave the lips lightly touching.**

2) **Check your eyes are not fixed. Imagine your eyes are windows and let the light bounce of this page into the back of your head.**

3) **Sense the movement of air in an out of your nostrils, but don't try to suck it in.**

4) **Look around you while staying aware of your lips, eyes and nose.**

5) **Think 'soft face'.**

Try this in activities away from your game and see what difference it makes to the movement. This can also be used in the rest of these experiments.

3. The Bookkeeper

When you place your hands on the club, do you also lift your shoulders or clench your jaw? It may only be by a fraction, but as soon as you do this you're using muscles that are inappropriate to the task – and reducing the sensitivity of your hands. What about when you use a keyboard? Or when you drive or hold a book?

 This can help to sensitise your hands with obvious benefits for your grip.

1) **Stand with your arms by your side and hold a book in each hand. An average-sized paperback is fine.**

2) **Be aware of the contact of your fingertips on the books.**

3) **Soften your face as in the previous experiment and let that work its way through your neck, shoulders, arms and palms of the hands and allow your grip to loosen by relaxing your forearms.**

4) **See how much tension you can release from your grip while still supporting the books.**

5) **Now let one hand at a time release so you eventually drop the book.**

How much tension could you release and yet still find it was sufficient to keep the book in your hand? Was the initial amount of effort you thought necessary well in excess of the actual amount requirement for the task? When you take hold of your club, check you haven't 'made a face' and tightened your jaw. Keep your forearms relaxed and be aware of all of the parts of your fingers and palms that are making contact with the grip.

4. Floating Arms

We've discussed the tendency of lifting the shoulders when preparing to swing. This is due to a misconception of how the shoulder joints function, due to repetition of poor movement. If you lift the whole shoulder when using your arm, you'll be using muscles to hold them up when they should be relaxed for your shot.

 This is one of my favourites.

1) **Stand with your arms resting by your sides.**

2) **Imagine two balls of air are floating up into the palms of your hands. (See Fig 7.2 over the page.)**

3) **Now visualise the balls of air expanding upwards into the gap between your arms and body and then outwards so your light arms start to lift slowly.**

4) **Be aware of the contact of the floor under your feet and imagine you're getting taller as your arms continue to lift *without* your shoulders lifting.**

You can experience this movement in a more 'mechanical' way by standing in a door way and pressing the backs of your hands into the frame for about twenty seconds before stepping forward. Your arms will then fly up without you feeling you've done the movement.

Fig 7.2 Think 'light arms' and let them rise without feeling you've done it yourself. Using 'light arms' when taking hold of your club will help keep your shoulders and neck free from unnecessary tension.

5. The Diamond

It's common to see people narrowing across the front of their torso when preparing to swing or putt. Pulling your shoulders forward and down reduces the flexibility of your torso for the rotation needed for your swing or for the pendulum action for the putt. In addition, the movement of your ribcage will be restricted at the very moment when demand for oxygenated blood from your muscles is at a premium.

 Pretty straight forward this one. Works well with the previous technique.

1) **You can do this either sitting or standing, but not while in your stance just yet.**

2) **Let your arms rest by your sides; run through steps 2 and 3 from the previous experiment.**

3) **Picture a diamond on the front and back of your shirt.**

4) **Let your arms lift slightly and then bring them around to the front; bring your palms lightly together without squashing or pulling the diamond out of shape.**

You can do this when reaching for your steering wheel, holding a book, using a keyboard or eating your lunch. See how often you find yourself unnecessarily rounding your shoulders.

6. The Monkey

This shallow squat, when done correctly, sets you up in a 'position of mechanical advantage' or, in other words, a stance that allows for the most efficient use of your body. It's a stance used in many sports as a ready position, for example, a tennis player facing a serve and, of course, a golfer preparing to take a shot. Although the squat stance does take your centre of gravity closer to the ground, you should avoid using a downward, pulling motion to get into it.

A good squat is 'springy', never fixed, and provides an excellent base for movement in any direction. If you think of it as a downward movement you'll tighten your hamstrings and your lower back when getting into it. This wipes out any mechanical advantage you may have had, restricts the power for your swing and reduces the sensitivity required for your putt. A poor stance also places additional stress on your body and increases the risk of injury.

The exercise on the next page is a based on a procedure used in The Alexander Technique. We call it 'Monkey' simply because it's how a monkey stands – plus life's too short to keep referring to it as 'the position of mechanical advantage'. When you perform this, don't think of it as getting into your golf stance just yet. Remember, the objective is to allow something different to happen, so we don't want any habits associated with your golf techniques appearing at this stage.

Please take your time with this one. A good *Monkey* can do wonders for your golf. Bet you've not heard that before!

1) Stand with your feet a little wider than your usual standing position and be aware of the contact you're making with the floor.

2) Think of unzipping the muscles across the base of your skull and allow you head to release a fraction forward.

3) At the same time, think of a space opening up in front of your ankles, behind your knees and in front of your hips.

4) Now send your torso back and up slightly, your hip joints away from your knees and release the muscles at the front of your thighs.

5) Your head should lead your lengthening torso forward and up, your legs will release and you should now be standing like a monkey with your arms resting in front of you.

6) Stay in this position for a minute and keep the whole body relaxed and poised with your head going away from your feet and your feet going away from your head.

It's vital to think of the whole process as an upward motion to take the weight off your legs, so they can release and stay 'springy'. Practise this up against a wall and you'll sense an upward movement of your pelvis as you adopt your stance. (See Fig 7.3 over the page.)

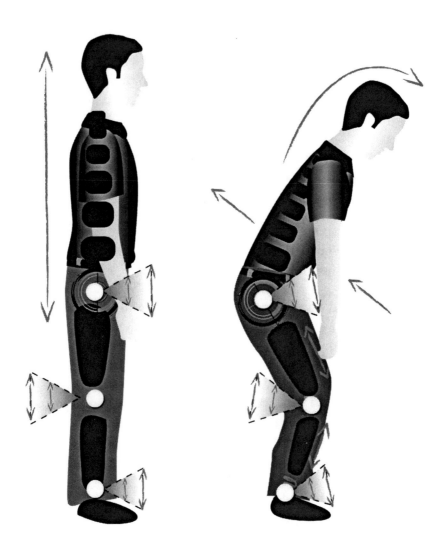

Fig 7.3 When performed correctly this movement will feel like it's happening by itself once you release your neck, hip, knee and ankle joints.

7. The Twist

We've talked about the importance of timing for golf and the danger of trying to do too much and interfering with your natural coordination. The movement in this experiment is not intended to replicate your swing but to give you an experience of twisting without tightening or 'corkscrewing' down into the ground.

Power comes from the unimpeded coordination of different parts of your body – with your head, neck, arms, torso and legs working together to create the momentum to drive the ball.

 When performing this movement, imagine you're getting taller as you turn, but beware of tightening anything to do it. Just think it.

1) **Stand with your feet slightly wider than for your standing posture and be aware of the contact you're making with the floor. Appreciate the push coming back up. When you start the movements below, imagine you're getting taller so you don't 'screw down' into the floor.**

2) **Let your eyes start to move to the left and allow your head to turn slowly following the movement, but don't let the shoulders move yet.**

3) **When your head has reached the end of its rotation, allow your shoulders to move to the left. Keep the thought that the floor is pushing up and you can release upwards as you rotate.**

4) **Once your shoulders have moved as far as they can, let your pelvis start to move. Keep moving in this**

upwards rotation until you feel your feet need to move. Stop there.

5) Maintain this position for a few moments and then release to untwist. Get a sense of letting the different parts of your body find their own way back to their rightful place – rather than putting them back to where you think they should sit.

6) Repeat on the opposite side. You may find one side is easier than the other. Most of us have a slight twist in the spine due to our repetitive activities. If it feels harder on one side, it's because you're going against your twist.

Now try performing a practice swing with the same sensation of twisting without pulling yourself down. Think 'release up'. Note: this doesn't involve coming up out of your stance. Instead, it's about keeping the distance between the top of your head to the soles of you feet, so you don't pull down.

From The Lab To The Course

Experiments are purely academic unless you get some practical benefit from them. When you're next on the golf course, think about how you're standing, walking and lifting your club from your bag and then observe how you get set to play your shot. Notice how much effort you want to use and see if you can reduce this and let your body flow. If you always do things in the same manner, you may never find your optimum swing, putt or chip shot.

Learn to detach yourself from the outcome and think like a scientist. Be curious; be prepared to try things out that you'd normally expect *not* to work. You may be pleasantly surprised. Many of the best discoveries have been made by accident.

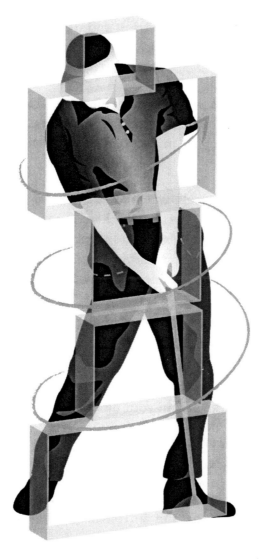

Fig 7.4 If you release and rotate without pulling down, the movement will be easier to coordinate. Note, this does not mean coming up from your stance.

Playing In The Zone [7] – *Awareness in Action*

The key to getting into the moment and ultimately The Zone is to be aware of yourself being totally involved in the action. This means being conscious that 'this is me playing this shot now'.

When you watch a movie you'll alternate from being totally absorbed in what's happening on the screen and being distracted by something happening in the 'real' world – unless it's a really good movie!

Being aware of yourself watching the screen while taking in what's happening in the movie keeps you in the moment. However, in this example being in the moment defeats the reason for watching the movie in the first place, that is, some harmless escapism. You'll have to decide what's best for you on the course.

 Here's a game you can play at home. All you need is a plastic or practice ball and a bucket.

1) **Place the bucket about six feet away and either stand or sit with the ball in your hand.**

2) **Think one or two of our *Getting into The Moment Thoughts*. (See page 111.)**

3) **Aim to throw the ball into the bucket and, in your 'mind's eye', feel the movement of your arm and see the arc of the ball.**

4) **Stay relaxed, breathe, aim and then move to throw – and be conscious of the moment you choose to let go of the ball. Watch it without caring where it lands.**

5) Repeat the throw while being aware that 'this is me throwing the ball at the bucket'. If you miss, stay relaxed, make adjustments, and continue. See if your reaction can stay the same regardless of whether you hit or miss.

6) Observe both your own movement and that of the ball.

7) Change the distance and repeat.

You can use a similar process when chipping. Be aware of the movement of your arms, hands and club as you perform your backswing, swing and follow-through. Watch the arc of the ball with a mind that you're controlling where it's going to land.

8 Stepping Up To The Zone

I believe being in the moment is the route for getting into The Zone. I used to think they were both the same state, whereas now I see The Zone as the next stage on from being in the moment. We go from being totally absorbed in an activity to suddenly firing on all cylinders with a sense of euphoria as every sinew of our being is united in achieving a goal. Yes, it sounds pretty dramatic, but that's how every sports person I've spoken to relates to it.

When you're in The Zone it's an absolute joy, whether you're playing golf or walking the dog. For that reason alone every person should make it a priority to aspire to reach it. From a sporting point of view it's the best way, in my view, to a peak performance. Every thought is focused entirely on the task in hand, and every action is carried out with absolute precision and with ease. You don't even really have to think about what you're doing because it seems so simple and the most natural thing to do.

You've probably experienced it before, but do you know how you got there? For most people it's almost accidental when we suddenly find ourselves there. The procedures in this book will help you perfect a process that can get you into the moment more often, opening up the way into The Zone. It does require a little more focus for golfers, due to the nature of the sport; you just have to treat the walk between shots and observing your partners play as part of your game to get into the moment.

From a skill point of view, being in the moment heightens your self-awareness. I spoke earlier about Mr Perfect – that annoying chap who can play anything without having to try. He's naturally in the moment and therefore learns so much quicker.

In the absence of all the superfluous actions the rest of us add for good measure, he keeps his technique simple with minimal activity through good coordination. In short, this means he's doing less that can go wrong. Once you learn to be in the moment you'll have an advantage over Mr Perfect, because you'll know why and how the process works. If he ever loses this ability (and we can but hope) he won't know how to get it back, because he's never learned the skill in the first place.

And Relax...

I see getting into the moment as a similar process to falling asleep. If you try to 'do it' it won't happen. To fall asleep all you need are the right conditions – a dark room, a warm, comfortable bed, a clear mind and the rest takes care of itself. If at any stage you become conscious of the process of drifting off, you'll come back to full consciousness and have to start all over again.

In sport the conditions that enable us to get into the moment are all there. Mihaly Csikszentmihalyi, a professor of psychology and authority on The Zone, believes that if the following are present in any activity, it's possible to enter into it.

1) **The presence of a challenging activity.** You're standing 425 yards from a small hole in the ground that you can't even see. There's a ball in front of you sitting on a piece of plastic and you have to get it into that hole using a long stick in four shots or under. Enjoy the challenge, be creative and produce something spectacular. Even if it goes pear-shaped you'll still have learned something in the process.

2) The perception that your skills match the challenge.
We're not just talking golfing skills here. If you practise these techniques you'll have the ability to control your thinking and hone your observational skills to play closer to your optimum each day. As your golf improves you'll feel you can play a greater role in controlling more and more of the actions you take to make the ball do what you want it to. It's immensely pleasurable to carefully plan and execute something to achieve a target – and know exactly how you did it.

3) Clear goals. Well, it couldn't be clearer, could it? The ball has to go down the hole. But when you're in the moment, that particular goal is some way off when you're at the tee. For each moment you have a clear goal. To stay in the moment is a goal. To get into your stance in the moment is a goal. To view the ball and not think of hitting it just yet is another goal. To be aware of your touch on the club handle without lifting your shoulders is yet another. A clear concept of the goal for each moment helps you achieve more.

4) The availability of instant feedback concerning your performance. The position of the ball instantly feeds back what you've just done. This allows you to modify your technique to cope with the unique conditions of the day. This also brings the skill aspect back into the equation as you can take pleasure in seeing your consciously-worked-out adjustments to your technique bring about the desired results.

The conditions are present; all you have to do is to let yourself become immersed in what you're doing, whether walking to the tee, lining up your shot or standing over the ball – and you'll drift into The Zone. But be wary of trying too hard because you'll stop the process before it's even started.

It doesn't have to be a sport or even a challenging activity. Csikszentmihalyi found that factory workers on a production line could experience the high of The Zone. A round of golf offers the ideal circumstances plus the added benefit of fresh air. However, anxiety about missing a shot or trying too hard to get it right can prevent you from achieving the presence of mind that will start the ball rolling into The Zone — and the hole. Dr Patrick J. Cohn, a sports psychologist, coaches sports people to 'release a bad play', so it doesn't interfere with the rest of their game. If the last shot is still on your mind, whether good or bad, it will prevent you from being in the moment and will usually affect your next shot.

A recent study by Flegal and Anderson found that skilled players who thought or talked about how they played their last shot in between strokes were more likely to perform the next one badly. They believe that 'reflecting consciously on what one knows about a skill often undermines its proper execution'. This effect is known as 'verbal overshadowing': the brain becomes 'confused' about the best way to carry out the task if we verbalise how it's to be done.

I believe 'verbal overshadowing' will also prevent you from getting into The Zone, because you may be trying too hard. Words are enough to trigger habitual reactions that, in turn, can take you out of the moment. Away from golf you can experience this while using a keyboard. You may be able to tap away quite fast, automatically allowing your fingers to find the right keys, but as soon as you start to think about what you're doing it slows up the whole process. We can prevent this overshadowing effect by not focusing on the skill but, instead, upon the 'body basics' that lie beneath your technique. You may need to verbalise them initially, but after a while you'll find it develops into a single image or word that you normally wouldn't associate with your golfing skills, for example, 'soft jaw'.

Getting Down To Business

So, to get into The Zone you first have to get into the moment. To get into the moment you have to focus on the activity in hand. The important issue here is to decide: *What is the actual activity to focus on*? Isn't that obvious? It's golf! Well, actually that's not quite how it works. Your golfing technique is the end product of a multitude of activities such as standing, walking, bending, twisting and gripping. To get into the moment you have to take a step back from your technique to be truly focused on the present.

Let's walk through the process out on the course.

Step 1: The Casual Observer

When you're standing waiting to tee-off, you're doing exactly that – standing. You're also breathing and watching the golfer in front. You can spend this time getting into the moment using some of the suggestions coming up so you're ready once the action starts. Try the following the next time you're waiting at the tee. You don't have to do them all, but you may find a combination of one or two work well for you. I mentioned some of these earlier and I've added a few more for you to try. You may come up with more of your own, but remember to keep it relevant.

These are our *Getting into The Moment Thoughts.* Be aware of:

- **Your toes in your socks (but don't wiggle them)**

- **The ground under your feet**

- **The touch of your clothes on your skin**

- The movement of your ribs as you breath

- The movement of air in and out of your nose

- The touch of your lips on each other

- The gap between your upper and lower teeth

- The breeze on your face

- The images in front of you coming *into* your eyes

- The actions of other golfers – but don't judge!

With practice you'll still be able to talk to your fellow players while maintaining a sense of some of the above. Although this initially seems quite a lot to think about, it can bring about an inner stillness with no real discernible effort. This helps to remove tension, free up your movement and aid concentration. You're now in a calm, focused state once it's your turn to line up your shot.

So what happens now? When you're ready to play you have another challenge. You really don't want to try to get it right.

Step 2: The Detached Golfer

Who Cares Wins? It may sound counterproductive, but you really shouldn't care what's going to happen once you start to line up your shot. Stay detached from the result and you'll be in a better state of mind to make the best decisions about how to play the shot in front of you. You're also still in the moment. Many players comment that their practice swing usually feels better than the actual shot. This is because they're not concerned about hitting the ball yet. They'll be in the moment of purely performing the swing.

When you add the ball into the equation you're adding something extra that could interfere with your technique. Even the slightest apprehension about the ball can affect your shot as your muscles will only be too happy to react to your anxious thoughts. If you 'care' about the outcome, you'll invariably try too hard and bring mostly unnecessary actions into the shot. Ever noticed how sometimes you play a great shot when you're trying not to? For instance, when you try *not* to sink a long putt to beat your boss?

Obviously your objective is to get the ball into the hole eventually, otherwise you may as well not bother. Sports Psychologist, Dr Bob Rotella, suggests that, although you should focus on a specific target initially, you then commit the target to your 'mind's eye' once you start to prepare for taking the shot. Decide on where you want it to land and then let go of that thought. You've made up your mind and set yourself up to play the shot, anything else you bring to it at this point will more than likely interfere. Visualising where the ball will land can take some of the work you think you have to do out of the shot.

Remember, the more you try to do, the more there is to get wrong.

If you're concerned about getting it right at this point, you'll be out of the moment and thinking about what's yet to happen. So by now you've chosen your club, lined up the shot and are now addressing the ball. In *this* particular moment you're:

- **Just looking at the ball**

- **Not swinging**

- **Breathing slowly**

- **Satisfied you've done the right preparation**

- **Holding the right club for the distance and shot**

- **Lined up for the shot**

You really don't have to think about landing in the right place as that's already taken care of. Just stay focused and look out for those unnecessary habitual actions; if one appears, say *no* and go back a step. When you're poised and happy, say your *now* word (see Playing In The Zone [5] on page 59) and start your backswing.

Try hitting a few balls on the driving range without giving a thought to where it's going. See if it helps to free up your swing and send the ball a few extra yards. Once you can do this, have half a thought to aim at a particular spot but don't allow yourself to care whether you land in it or not.

Being detached and indifferent to the result can free up your muscles, remove anxiety and open up your senses.

Step 3: The Cool Analyst

So now you've played your shot and noted where it's landed without a hint of satisfaction or frustration – well, maybe only a trace, let's be realistic! But seriously, you'll need to note the outcome of your actions and also how the unique conditions of the day played their part.

If you can stay in the same detached state in which you prepared and played the shot, you'll be able to make better observations and draw more accurate conclusions from what just happened – by not letting pride get in the way.

> To be elated at success and disappointed at failure is to be a child of circumstances; how can such a one be called a master of himself.
> Chinese Proverb

Stand tall, keep the ground under your feet, keep breathing and do your analysis.

Step 4: The Sunday Walker

Now, momentarily forget about what just happened and use the walk to stay in the moment, free up your legs, shoulders and back, and enjoy the scenery (see Body Basics [5] on page 80). Once you arrive at the ball you can go back to Step 1 and repeat the process. The more you stay in the moment the better your chances of stepping up into The Zone. When you get into The Zone you can forget about doing all of this until you find yourself back out of it.

You know when you're in The Zone when —

You're fully aware of everything around you without any effort on your part.

You almost know how things are going to turn out.

Life is good.

Everything is easy.

Things seem to happen by themselves.

You find yourself smiling.

You don't have to care about what your ball is doing.

You're having a great time.

But be careful out there! If you become aware you're in The Zone, *don't* do anything to try and stay there because you'll drop straight back out. Just keep enjoying the moment and let nature run its course.

Eating Your Way To The Zone

Top golfers don't use sports nutritionists just so they can look good on the course – at least I don't think they do. What you eat plays a huge part in your performance and also whether you get into The Zone or not.

Eating a large takeaway stuffed with additives, sugar and various other unmentionables is not the best preparation for a round of golf, or anything else for that matter. Aside from the obvious consideration of energy input and release, it is also known that certain substances found in foods help release neurotransmitters within the brain. For instance, phenylalanine found in meat, eggs, grains and soybeans is used to process dopamine, a neurotransmitter that affects brain processes controlling movement, emotion and the ability to experience pain and pleasure. Tryptophan found in meat, dairy, bananas and eggs is involved in the manufacture of serotonin, the feel good neurotransmitter. The production of dopamine and serotonin is thought to increase when athletes experience The Zone.

There are over one hundred thousand chemical reactions occurring in the brain every second, so balance is vital. Perhaps you've experienced a time when you got this wrong when training after a heavy meal or eating junk food. You may have had a sense of feeling lethargic, having little energy and no ability to focus.

Your chances of getting into The Zone can be greatly enhanced by eating the right foods. However, every individual responds differently to the same food, so it is worth getting professional advice from a sports nutritionist or experimenting to find what works for you.

Tom's Predicament — Part Four

Tom has 're-educated' himself away from his golf using the experiments with movement and focus from this and the previous chapters. He now has a better understanding of his body and how his thoughts influence movement. This brings a new level of control over his actions, way above his previous ability.

He's now ready to take this into his game as his newfound level of awareness, or 'radar', will pick up and recognise the majority of the previous unnecessary, habitual actions that are likely to spoil the shot.

When it comes to getting out on the course, he'll appreciate how he developed his bad habit in the first place. He can stay focused on each current task, that is, stay in the moment and prevent the unwanted muscular reactions he associated with his previous technique. For example, when he prepares for his shot, he has to *not* think of hitting the ball because the very thought will trigger his old habit of tightening his shoulders.

He has learned to stay in the moment, not get too far ahead of himself and prevent the actions he has yet to perform from interfering with what's currently required.

To consolidate what he's learned and to continue to develop his ability, he can use the experiments in movement and awareness in this book. In the last part of the book we'll step into his mind as he plays a few shots, so you can see how it has all come together.

Playing In The Zone [8] – **Breathe Easy**

Breathing is something we have to do. We do it in our sleep, on the golf course and even while having a conversation. It's pretty much an automatic process – but one we can interfere with drastically if we try to breathe 'properly'. You can do the following procedure standing, sitting or lying down.

To get into the moment you're going to focus on the activity, but you're *not* to think of breathing as the activity. This is based on a procedure that Alexander (F.M. Alexander, founder of the technique bearing his name) called the *Whispered Ah* which is popular with singers and performing artists.

 Try this sitting, standing or while in your stance with your club.

1) **Be aware of the movement of air in and out of your nose.**

2) **Notice the movement of your ribs as your lungs inflate and deflate.**

3) **For a few moments just let yourself be 'breathed' as changes in air pressure do it all for you. Take a back seat and observe where the ribs are moving. Note: there should be only a slight pause between the inhalation and exhalation phase. If there is a long gap, you're interfering with the free-flow of air.**

4) **Let your mouth drop slowly open and exhale adding a slight whisper to it. When you reach the point where the flow starts to dip (don't empty your lungs!), close your mouth and do absolutely nothing.**

5) After a brief pause the air will begin to flow back in through your nose and push the ribs out and up slightly. You do not need to attempt to move your ribs as the incoming air inflating your lungs will push them out. If you try to move your ribs, it will interfere with your coordination.

6) Return to 'normal' breathing and repeat the 'whisper breath' every few minutes. Listen to the sound of your whisper – it should sound like a gas leak. Undue tension in your body will alter the sound.

I asked you to focus on the movements and not to think of this as breathing, because breathing is not the activity. It's too tempting to try to *do* the breathing by sucking in air and pushing out the stomach as soon as we think about it.

If the ribs aren't moving you're holding tension somewhere in your frame and causing the muscles of the torso to act like a straight jacket. You don't need to suck air in. It will flow in automatically due to the lower pressure in your lungs. Your nose is the way in to your lungs and should remain passive in the breathing process.

You can use a shortened version of this on the golf course using a sigh – as I doubt you'll want to be standing on the course with your mouth wide open catching flies. This can help release tension before you play your shot and also help you into the moment. You can also use this procedure on a practice swing. If you're relaxed, the flow of air will remain constant throughout.

9 Seize The Moment

Every player occasionally suffers from a loss of confidence, poor form, problems with a specific shot or injury. The way to fulfilment is beset with many bunkers, some just as easy to get out of as they were to get in, whereas others are deeper, less easy to spot and therefore harder to negotiate. When you find yourself in a spot of bother, your resourcefulness will be tested and your strengths and weaknesses exposed. How you cope with these obstacles defines you both as a golfer and person. A crisis is best dealt with in a clear and calm state of mind. When you can see the bigger picture, your observations, decisions and subsequent actions are more likely to be the right ones. But while it's easier to see the fish in calm waters, you still have to catch them.

Let's have a look at some of the likely situations you may find yourself in.

A Bad Day At The Office

If you're having one of those days when it's just not happening, how do you change it there and then on the golf course? It doesn't help when someone tells you to 'chill out, it's only a game'. Is it heck! Of course, getting frustrated or annoyed at yourself isn't going to help, but it's difficult not to react negatively when silly mistakes are spoiling your round. But a bad day is just that – a bad day. You'll be better next time. Even if you're in the middle of a competition, there are positive steps you can take to improve the situation.

Adding more stress to your game by being over-critical and trying harder to correct it will simply reinforce your current behaviour and worsen the situation.

Research by John Toner at University College Dublin found that when golfers feel under pressure and focus more on their technique, they actually make matters worse. He found those who placed their attention away from their technique often got better results. This could include thinking about the hole or a part of the green, as long as they didn't concentrate on their technique.

So, what can you do to change your current fortune? Here are a few tips. Some may sound like the last thing you should be thinking but, remember, if banging your head against a brick wall isn't working, don't bang it any harder!

- **Stop caring about how the game is going.**

- **Don't try to play correctly – you've been doing that already and it's not working.**

- **Stop trying so hard – have a passing interest in where you'd like the ball to go and leave it at that.**

- **Be amused at your situation.**

- **Tell yourself you're going to enjoy the next shot.**

- **Take in the scenery; would you really want to be anywhere else?**

The objective is to break out of the loop you're stuck in that's preventing your natural game from flowing. If you can use the odd bad day to discard your pride and try something different, you'll prevent the blip becoming a dip.

Form Has Left The Building

If at first you don't succeed – give up! This may sound like something Homer Simpson would say but it's actually very good advice. Okay, the 'give up' bit doesn't mean selling your clubs on eBay; it means stop doing what you're doing, go back a few steps and find another way. If what you're doing isn't working, it doesn't make sense to keep trying in the same way only harder.

Form is an interesting yardstick. Obviously your scores tell you in black and white how well you're doing, but we also have a more subjective view of how we feel we're performing. Form is different to skill. You'll have a level of skill that should constantly be on an upward curve, whereas form is your ability to apply your skills on a daily basis – and this can be quite fragile.

One day you're playing quite happily and then suddenly something goes wrong and dents your confidence. Maybe you missed an absolute sitter or shanked the ball; whatever you've done it can still be on your mind for the next shot or when you're back out again. Before you know it you're suffering a full-blown loss of form with the danger of losing your confidence in your ability altogether. This highlights the importance of playing in the moment and being able to 'release a bad play' with a pro's skill for 'instant amnesia'.

What if you're already in a trough? How do you get your form back?

Again, it's important to put it into some sort of context. Players of every sport have suffered from a loss of form at some stage of their career. Most will get through it unscathed. Yes, a minority won't, but the smart players will see it as an opportunity to reassess their technique and emerge a much-improved player with a better understanding of their game. You may feel the need to find out exactly what led to your sudden demise, but I believe this can complicate matters. For a start, it may have been an external influence that was to blame – and nothing to do with your ability. If you respond as if you were at fault, you're heading off on a totally unnecessary course of action. On the other hand, what may appear to be the obvious cause could purely be a symptom of something deeper (but not necessarily darker!). Even if you do successfully identify the cause, how are you going to rectify it?

Playing in the moment is the best way to avoid this sort of trap and is also the best way to get out of it. Habits are easy to learn but harder to break. If you take the approach that you have to do something more or extra to get your form back, you may complicate matters. Trying means extra effort, and extra effort usually isn't a good thing. Just a tiny amount of inappropriate tension in a muscle you're using to correct a perceived problem will soon become a permanent part of your technique. Your 'solution' could have complicated your technique and taken you further away from your natural game.

A loss of form is, in my experience, usually down to the fact you've started to do something extra rather than stopped doing something.

It may be quite a small thing that has slowly crept into your technique. You won't have noticed it initially, because it's become woven into your game and it's insignificant enough not to make a huge difference. But, just like the experience of the unfortunate camel and the last straw, the scales tip and suddenly it goes wrong. A loss of form can have its origin in a moment long before it comes to your attention.

A good place to start to get your form back is to work on the principle that 'less is more'. Approach it as if you have to *stop* doing something – and you'll be on the right track. Onions usually get a mention in this situation because it's a good analogy. To allow you natural game to return, or even show itself for the first time, you need to peel away the outer layers of the onion and remove all the unnecessary bits you've unknowingly brought to your game. Use the procedures from this book to discover where you've been doing something unnecessary and see what happens when you remove it. Do this with an open mind and it won't end in tears.

Some of the world's greatest discoveries have been made in a state of quiet contemplation. Einstein claimed his best ideas came to him while he was taking a walk away from his study. The more you can play in a state of stillness the more you'll notice the slight daily variations that may be affecting your form.

Going Back To The Drawing Board

If you've always had difficulties with a specific aspect of your game, you'll need to start again. This is where being able to break your reliance on old habits will pay dividends. Remember, your existing technique will feel as familiar and comfortable as an old pair of shoes. Even if you're struggling with a particular shot, you'll still want to prepare to play it the same way each time because it feels right. What you're actually doing is setting yourself up to repeat the conditions that lead to the unwanted result. If you build a house on poor foundations it will collapse. You can continue to rebuild it, but it will never be up to the job if you don't sort the foundations out first.

If you've never been happy with your swing, you really need to start again and build it back up from the ground. Don't start thinking about changing it once you're in your stance because this is too late. You'll already have put in place all the cues that make you do whatever it is that's spoiling the shot.

So what can you do if something is just not working? Ask your playing partners? Go for some sessions with a pro? Reach for a book? Whatever approach you take, success comes down to making the correct diagnosis of the cause before you can start working on the solution.

Correcting a technical aspect of your game is a three-step process. If you get any one of the steps wrong it won't work.

Step 1. Identify the cause.

Step 2. Work out a plan of action.

Step 3. Successfully apply your plan.

STEP 1 is the most important part. It sounds easy enough, but if you identify the wrong cause you'll never correct the problem. Even if you see some improvement, the original problem will re-appear in a more complex form later. But surely it shouldn't be too difficult to find the cause of a technical difficulty? The clue is in the question. We're looking for a *cause* that is invariably not the obvious outward sign — because that's just the symptom. The real cause will not be visible to the naked eye because it's in your head. It's your concept of what's required to perform the technique that determines how you do it. Either your concept is wrong, and therefore you're never going to get it right, or your concept is correct but it's lost in translation on the way to your muscles.

Now that you've been using the procedures in this book, you may already have found a number of unnecessary actions that you're adding to your technique. Reliance on your habits makes the culprit harder to find. The familiarity of your actions will mean many will go unnoticed, and therefore you're trying to diagnose the problem with vital information missing.

To get a full picture you need to get into the moment, focus on your preparation and look for the usual suspects such as clenching your jaw, tightening your grip, stiffening your neck or lifting your shoulders – and let them go. Get a coach to watch or video your technique; a third party observer will see any number of actions (symptoms) that you haven't.

If someone points out something you weren't aware of, and this may be something as trivial as lifting your eyebrows before you swing, find out what it is that makes you want to do it. What's going through your mind when it happens? What are you attempting to do? How are you attempting to do it? The only way to find if this is the cause of your difficulty is to go through the following steps 2 and 3 and see what happens. If it doesn't resolve the problem, you start the process again.

STEP 2 could be as simple as stopping what you've discovered you were doing in the first step and, hey presto, result! You'll wonder why you struggled with it in the first place and why it's taken this long to resolve. This is a good example of what's possible when you can take a step back and observe what's really happening – and not rely on your habits.

However, this step could involve more than just checking your preparation. If you've had a less than efficient technique for any period of time, your movement may be compromised due to poor coordination; limited hip rotation is a good example. Using too much effort will have increased the amount of activity in those muscles not technically required for that particular movement. The effect is to put on the brakes. If this is the case, your plan needs to include an element of re-education. This will allow you to sense an easier, different way to move, without the effort you've become conditioned to use. Conveniently the procedures in this book will do this for you.

STEP 3 involves a trial and error loop, but even if it takes ten attempts you'll still learn something with each repetition. As the persistent entrepreneur would say, *'I haven't failed one hundred times, I've just found one hundred ways that don't work'*.

If the first step has highlighted that you're doing something unnecessary in your preparation, it may be hard to tell yourself not to do it. It's difficult to change just one bit of your technique in isolation because it's part of an overall pattern. If you tighten your grip just before you swing, it's because it's become an integral part of your preparation, so you won't think of starting your shot until you feel all of the sensations you associate with it. You may tighten your grip because you've clenched your jaw slightly, so it's this that needs to change.

Playing in the moment with a 'quiet mind' lowers the level of background noise in your nervous system and exposes activity that has previously been drowned out by the din. You'll start to notice every little thing you're doing with your body and therefore be able to stop and take control. This gives you a head start and, literally, lets you spot the stimuli coming, so you have time to prevent your usual response. At each stage of your preparation you can ask yourself whether you need to be doing what you feel you have to – and then make an informed decision to stop if necessary.

By breaking the first link in the chain you'll stop yourself heading off down the well-trodden path to your questionable technique. You'll allow something new to emerge.

Adding Insult To Injury

That sudden twinge in your lower back has probably been a long time in the making. Our bodies are very good at adapting to the demands we put upon them, but unfortunately they're also susceptible to poor conditioning. If your techniques contain inefficient movements, you'll be placing undue stress on parts of your body and eventually something will give. The maverick Australian running coach Percy Cerutty would tell his athletes, "If you can hear the whispers you never have to hear the screams."

You can do a lot to prevent complications if you get help as soon as you hear a whisper. Don't be tempted to ignore aches and pains and play through them, because they'll only come back big time later. Firstly, visit a physiotherapist, chiropractor, osteopath or sports masseur for an assessment. Manipulation can help to free up movement of joints that may be inflamed by poor technique or overuse. If your range of movement in just one joint in your body is limited, other joints will have to compensate, and as your movement becomes compromised the situation can only get worse. You may also consider getting a podiatry biomechanical assessment. Golf orthotics can help to correct alignment that could be causing difficulties with your technique and leading to injury.

Manual treatment is however only half the solution. What have you been doing to cause the problem in the first place? If Tom drives his car badly for long enough, something will go wrong with it. The garage may be able to fix the mechanical fault but it won't change his driving habits. As soon as Tom drives away, the process starts all over again. To prevent injury or a recurrence of an old one you need to improve both your golfing techniques and how you use your body on a daily basis. Sitting and moving correctly when you're away from the golf course will help you when you're on it.

Maintaining focus as we sit at our computers, drive our cars in heavy traffic or slump on the couch can be a challenge. Once we get engrossed in our daily activities, we lose sense of the *how* we're doing and we cruise along at the mercy of our bad habits. We use the wrong muscles for the wrong actions, and coordination goes out of the window along with the natural poise we had in our youth. It should therefore be no surprise our body starts to complain when we take it out for a round of golf.

So how can you regain lost poise?

You won't be too surprised to hear that being in the moment has quite a large role to play in the process. This allows you to notice and let go of the excessive tension that's pulling your body out of shape. Your postural reflexes will then get a chance to coordinate your muscles accordingly with minimal effort, putting less stress on your muscles, joints, ligaments and tendons. Learn to apply the same awareness to your daily activities as you do for your golf, and both your game and body will benefit.

If you want to go down the re-education route further you might consider taking lessons in The Alexander Technique (my own discipline), Feldenkrais Method or Trager work. For more information, see Useful Resources on page 153.

Confidence And Paranoia

Sports Psychologists will tell you that a confident player is much more likely to succeed than one who lacks it. If you think positively, you'll get positive results. But what exactly is confidence and how do you attain it? When does confidence turn into complacency? Can you fake it or fool yourself into being confident?

Confidence is about knowing you have the skills to achieve the task in hand without being unreasonable about your objective. Setting impossible goals and failing to meet them isn't going to build confidence. Of course, this doesn't mean you can't work on improving your game, but do it intelligently by getting help and using the methods in this book to develop your timing, strength and accuracy.

Complacency is when you assume you have the skills – and also assume that's all that it takes to succeed.

Your confidence will grow as you learn how to make the ball go nearer to where you want it to go more often. Being in the moment and being conscious of exactly what you're doing with your body will allow you to take more control of the myriad of variables involved in making a successful shot. Anything that remains outside of your awareness is an 'unknown' and therefore beyond your control. Too many 'unknowns' leave too much to chance and erratic performance, and that doesn't make for a confident player.

You can invariably tell when a player is confident simply by observing their body language before they even play the shot. They stand tall with relaxed shoulders and they are the picture of poise with a free flowing, easy manner. Reverse all that and you'll see an anxious individual. A confident player has faith in their skill and ability to apply it, and hence will have no anxious thoughts seeping into their muscles.

If you're feeling confident, your posture exudes your mood and you'll look and feel good. If you look and feel good it can help to feed your confidence. It's a self-perpetuating process. But what if you're not feeling on top of your game? Can you kick-start a much needed confidence boost? I believe you can.

Use the practical exercise on page 83 (Balance Reflexes) and see what happens when your posture improves. It's impossible to split your mind from your body because without one you don't have the other. By altering your stance you'll change what you're feeling. The sensation of a strong, supple and poised body not only helps make us feel better, it also promotes free movement and increased self-awareness.

Getting A Grip

A few years ago I learned a very useful lesson while standing in a supermarket queue behind a mother and young boy of about three years. The boy was pleading with his mum for a chocolate bar (so thoughtfully placed at the checkout where a young child couldn't fail to see it). His mother was having none of it and, just as he contemplated unleashing a full-blown tantrum, she calmly but sternly said, "You're not getting any chocolate – now deal with it!" Although at the time I thought this was harsh advice for such a young lad, it epitomises what we need to do when things aren't going our way. Deal with it!

Throwing a tantrum or getting frustrated solves nothing and certainly won't help you to get into The Zone. The timely intervention from the boy's mother worked, and he opted to sulk instead; I made a mental note to try it with my kids. The mother effectively broke the link in the chain, with possibly the benefit of previous conditioning, and stopped the inevitable outcome.

Playing in the moment is like having an expert coach, or even your mother, talking calmly in your ear and bringing things to your attention that may have gone unnoticed – and therefore beyond your control. An incident that could have been the start of a crisis is now viewed as an opportunity to address an aspect of your game. This doesn't mean you won't need help from others, but you'll find it easier to assess and take on board their advice where appropriate. If you can accept the facts in front of you and take mature, intelligent action based on reliable evidence, you'll benefit from the many and varied challenges golf will throw at you. Cope with these and you'll come out of the other end a better, more rounded golfer.

Playing In The Zone [9] – **Armchair Zen Master**

How often do you get frustrated with yourself on the course? Are you annoyed or angered by colleagues at work? Whether on or off the course, events seemingly beyond our control can lead to frustration, anger and stress. However, although you cannot control everything happening in the world, you can control your response to them. Missing a simple putt is only frustrating if you let it frustrate you. Stress is your response to the situation; it's not the situation's fault if you react negatively.

You can try this practical exercise while viewing TV from the comfort of your armchair. It works even better if you're watching something that gets you involved, such as a sports event, political debate or scary movie.

 Who'd have thought you could improve your golf while watching TV?

1) **Place your hands on your legs or arms of the chair. Relax your hands and let the whole palm come into contact with what's underneath.**

2) **Give your hands a break and let them sit without doing anything. Sense the shape, texture and temperature of the surface beneath them, but don't move them.**

3) Do the same with your feet and maintain an awareness of both your hands and feet while watching TV.

4) Be aware of the movement of your ribs and the movement of air in and out of your nose and think 'soft face'.

5) Keep a sense of *'This is me watching TV'* and see if you can prevent yourself from reacting habitually to what's happening. Maybe you shout at the TV if your team is doing badly or if a politician has evaded the question yet again. Don't suppress your reaction; just let it go over your head so it doesn't invoke a response.

6) See how long you can sit in this detached state without reacting to the events on the box.

This process can work in all situations and is particularly useful when things aren't going well on the course or if you have teenagers in the family! Learning to detach yourself from your surroundings buys you time to choose how you respond, and it gets you into the moment by breaking the stimulus/response chains that bind you to your habits.

10 Taking It To The Next Level

Are you playing to your full potential? How would you know? You may feel you've reached the top of your game or that you're pretty close to the best you'll ever be. However, bear in mind that the advances you've made to date are based on your inherent habits that have set the limit of your achievements. If from day one your habitual patterns contained below-par movements, you could be playing below your true potential. For instance, you may be fairly satisfied with your swing, blissfully unaware that it's inefficient and that you're failing to hit the ball the full distance you're truly capable of.

Taking your game to the next level sounds exciting and desirable, but what is the next level? How do you get there and how do you know when you've got there? For me, the 'next level' represents a quantum leap following a eureka moment that brings with it a new understanding of the game. This comes from intelligent, focused practice and not just from blood, sweat and tears. In fact, I believe it's best to avoid the 'no pain, no gain' approach.

Are You Trying To Fail?

Improvements in performance can only come about from hard work. Really? Firstly, you have to know what you're going to focus all that hard work on and, secondly, whether your effort is applied in a way that will bring about the best results. Although it's good to have a goal, such as increasing the distance of your drive or improving your chip shot, it's important that these goals don't become the sole focus of your game.

The following story emphasises this point perfectly.

Old Japanese Proverb

A young boy travelled across Japan to the school of a famous martial artist. When he arrived at the school he was given an audience by the teacher.

"What do you wish from me?" the master asked.

"I wish to be your student and become the finest karate student in the land," the boy replied. "How long must I study?"

"Ten years at least," the master answered.

"Ten years is a long time," said the boy. "What if I studied twice as hard as all your other students?"

"Twenty years," replied the master.

"Twenty years! What if I practise day and night with all my effort?"

"Thirty years," was the master's reply.

"How is it that each time I say I will work harder, you tell me that it will take longer?" the boy asked.

"The answer is clear. When one eye is fixed upon your destination, there is only one eye left with which to find the Way."

Anon.

When you're fixed on achieving a goal, the blinkers can take the enjoyment out of your game. You may also add anxiety where it's not wanted and be prevented from experiencing those unlooked-for moments of enlightenment.

Striving to improve usually brings excessive effort as we try harder to gain our end. What do you do when you feel the need to *try harder*? How many times do you say to yourself on the golf course that you need to concentrate, try harder or focus on your technique?

You cannot achieve what you don't yet know purely by doing what you already know.

F.M. Alexander

What do you then do differently? When you 'try harder' you invariably add a bit more of what you're already doing. However, from my own experience, and from working with golfers, I would say you're likely to furrow your brow, fix your eyes and jaw, hold your breath, and tighten up a little for good measure. Test it out next time, I bet you'll do at least one of them! Do they help or are they going to make things worse?

The stereotypical 'trying harder' face is not good for promoting poise. Although these actions may convince us that we really are trying harder, we are in reality reducing our chances of a free, relaxed shot. Remember, your brain is only too happy to reproduce old, familiar patterns that will continue to reinforce your bad habits.

The more you try, the more your muscles will contract, reducing sensitivity and ultimately the control you have over your club. Take a few shots and see how little effort it takes, and let the club's momentum do the work for you. Also, notice how much more you become aware of when you remove even a small amount of unnecessary tension.

The Learning Zone

The Zone isn't just a great place to play, but also to learn. A whole new experience awaits you once you break free of the shackles of your performance-limiting habits. Until you hit a ball over 300 yards with little perceived effort, you won't be aware you can do it. If you keep slogging away day-in day-out with timing that sets half your effort against the other half, you'll continue to strengthen the concept of 'effort is good'. You may see the ball go further if you apply more force, but it would probably go even further still if you worked on your coordination.

When you're in The Zone, chemical activity in your brain helps optimise learning. Dopamine levels increase and speed up your data processing capacity, while rising alpha brain wave activity puts you into a state of 'relaxed wakefulness', ideal for attaining new skills and knowledge.

The most valuable lesson I believe we can learn in The Zone is that a peak performance comes from 'getting out of the way' and by not trying. It's no coincidence that artists refer to The Zone as 'The Flow'; it describes the process beautifully. We 'go with the flow', not against it. We get a sense of being carried along, while still being in control and not struggling to create the momentum. We're at our best when we're comfortably in control with no anxious thoughts about getting it right or improving performance.

Think back to your school days. Which lessons made the biggest impression? You were in The Zone on those days, so the process of learning wouldn't have felt like hard work at all. You would have felt comfortable with your teacher and under no pressure to learn. Those lessons are still with you now thanks to the combination of neurotransmitters and the strength of the neurons firing at the time. The relaxed, yet alert, state is perfect for understanding facts and storing a long-term memory. The same goes for a 'physical' memory of how to play at your peak.

Being able to set and achieve a goal following a logical, intelligent plan of action is immensely satisfying. To do it while enjoying every minute brings rewards beyond the usual sporting achievements. Playing golf is as much a part of your *personal* development as any other pursuit you have. The skills and abilities you attain from playing can help with your personal and professional life; it also works the other way around.

Into The Unknown

Never sit back and just be 'satisfied' with your game, thinking you've reached your peak or your limit. Instead, continue to spend time assessing your technique, your approach and even the reasons to why you play. This doesn't mean you have to get frustrated at any lack of progress. It simply means you need to keep an open mind and body — and you'll continue to develop your game.

If you think you've got it right, you'll try hard to keep producing that same result and you'll stagnate. Keep it fresh, new and challenging. Keep experimenting. Top players are where they are because they continually assess and make changes to their technique. How many times have Tiger Woods and Padraig Harrington changed their swing?

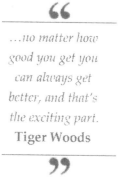

...no matter how good you get you can always get better, and that's the exciting part.
Tiger Woods

The next level is something you've yet to experience and therefore it's an unknown quantity. While you stay in the cosy surrounds of your comfort zone, you won't do anything new and challenging. If you bear in mind the quote from F. M. Alexander earlier, "*You cannot achieve what you don't yet know purely by doing what you already know*", then you'll appreciate the need to do something different to get to the next level. You can even play a few 'I don't give a damn' rounds – and you might surprise yourself.

You won't yet know what the next level has in store for you, or what it's going to feel like, so you really shouldn't focus on trying to get there. Keep playing in the moment, stay patient with your game and you'll get into The Zone more often – and then anything is possible!

You'll know when you get to the next level.

Playing In The Zone [10] – **One Small Step**

The objective with this next procedure is to practise stepping out of your comfort zone – literally. With this simple exercise you can practise coping with the uncertainty you'll face when trying something different on the golf course. If you can deal with this, you'll take a huge step away from what may be holding you back. You're going to take a step forward without doing any of the actions you may feel are necessary.

 Yes I know it sounds a bit dramatic but it's an interesting experience all the same.

1) **Stand and think of taking a step forward, but don't start to move.**

2) Observe what you want to do to get ready to step forward. Do you want to lean to one side? Are you starting to fall forward or hold your breath?

3) Try the rest of the practical exercise, but as soon as you feel one of your habitual actions is going to make an appearance, stop – and go back to step 1.

4) Let the knee of your leading leg bend and then roll onto the ball of your foot. Be aware of the push coming back from the floor. This will prevent you from shifting your weight onto the other leg.

5) Now think of your head leading your body up and forward over your leading leg, and let your foot come off the ground and swing through.

6) As you move forward your head will arrive over the bit of the floor where your foot will land.

You may experience a moment where you feel it's not possible to take the step, because none of the usual sensations you associate with it are present. Take a moment to get to know what it feels like to be unsure before performing an act you've done millions of times before – and then just let yourself take the step without caring what's going to happen.

11 Playing In The Zone

Young athlete: **"So how will I know when I'm in The Zone?"**

Coach: **"Oh, you'll know alright, don't you worry."**

The memories of a Zone moment will stay as fresh as if they happened yesterday and they can still bring joy many years later. I'm still dining out on some of mine from when I was 15! So, it's heart-breaking to hear someone who has played sport for many years say they've never experienced it. Others may have been there once or twice and regret never being able to recreate the sensation. Although some may say it's 'better to have loved and lost than never to have loved at all', it's better still to take frequent trips into The Zone.

Anxiety about your performance won't get you into The Zone. Is worrying about the shot going to help you one bit? As my grandmother used to say, "If the worst is going to happen anyway, there's no point worrying about it – and if it doesn't, then you've wasted all that time worrying." If it's going to stop you playing in The Zone then it's a crime!

In this last chapter we're going to listen in to Tom's thoughts as he plays the first hole in a county competition. We'll see how he prepares himself to get into The Zone by *not* trying to get there. Some of this may sound a little long-winded, and your first reaction may be that it seems just too much effort to put it into practice. However, a fraction of a second in Tom's mind can take quite a few words to describe, and many of his thoughts won't be verbalised at all but involve imagery. Besides, the reward is well worth it!

Whether you're aware of it or not, your mind is always active and maintains a constant dialogue with your muscles. It's just that most of this activity remains below your consciousness as you're either concentrating too much on something to the point of shutting out everything else, or day-dreaming with your mind drifting away with the fairies. What Tom is attempting to do here is to remain aware of every action – to get into the moment. Once he's in The Zone it happens automatically with no perceived effort. In fact, it's a joy to experience it.

So let's swallow the red pill and step into Tom's brain and listen in on his thoughts as he prepares to tee off at the first hole – a par 4 of 395 yards.

A Brief Moment In Tom

 "What a fabulous morning. The sun's shining, there's a slight breeze to keep the air fresh, and those clouds over there look like two sheep. The smell of the grass and the butterflies in my stomach take me back to standing at the start line on school sports day for the 60-metre sprint.

My heart's beating a little faster, the air's flowing in and out of my nose and I can feel my ribs moving under my arms against my shirt. I'm not nervous; I'm fired up ready to go.

This is why I play golf and this is why I enter these competitions. Everything I've done before has prepared me for this moment, and I'm ready to step up to this next challenge. I'm going to enjoy this. For the next few hours I'm going to live life to the full and let my skills do the talking. I don't have to try hard; I'll just get out of the way and let myself play how I know I can play.

Less is more; less is good.

Ian's going first so I'll stand here and enjoy the show for now. I've got a great view standing in front of the spectators. I bet there's not one of them who wouldn't want to be in my shoes, but I wouldn't swap this moment for anything. I'm ecstatic to be playing and I've earned the right to be standing on this spot today. Ian's looking good; it's going to be a challenge playing with him today.

My feet are relaxed and I can feel the gaps in between my toes. The ground is solid beneath me supporting and pushing back up, so I can release and just let my bones sit on one another. Shoulders. My shoulders have just dropped a fraction; I must have let the excitement get to them. They're relaxed now, but I'll keep an eye on them. Smell that grass. You can't beat this sensation on the first day of a competition. Yes, this is great. I feel ten feet tall, and nothing can stop me enjoying this day. Every fibre of my body is alert, on fire and working towards the same goal.

Stay detached, indifferent. I don't care what's going to happen because it won't help me one bit.

Now it's my turn. Let's show them what I can do.

I select my driver from the bag. I take it, hold it lightly with a soft wrist and feel its weight and walk to the tee. I feel tall and light and get a good spring from the ground under my feet. My jaw is relaxed and I let this go right through my body into my ankles, I let my legs release and place the tee and ball.

There's the spot where I want it to land – just to the right of that tall tree. Keep breathing, stay relaxed and line up the shot.

So, now I'm standing ready for my practice swing. I release up into my stance, legs as springs, space in front of my ankles, behind my knees and in front of my hips. I let these spaces open up and send my torso back and up release my legs. I'm in my poised stance now, free from tension – and it feels good. My hands are gripping the club handle, my forearms working my fingers to wrap around but not to tighten them.

I'm still breathing and feel my ribs moving into the space under my arms. Soften my jaw and let my teeth part a little. Oops, my head is dropping forward a little so I'll lengthen into the ground again and sense the push coming back up through my legs and spine. That's better. Now I can smile across the back of my head and let it release forward and up from the spine and let the release trickle down through my neck, shoulders and arms right to the ground.

I stay free in my stance as my springy legs grow into the ground and use the force coming back up, and I perform a practice swing. Wow, that felt good. I just took it to the top and then let the club head do the rest.

Ribs moving, air flowing in and out of my nose, I step up to the ball. Stay back from the club, keep breathing, lips lightly touching each other, hips, knees, ankles. I've got the right club for the distance. It's lined up and all taken care of, so I don't need to worry about a thing.

I'm not hitting the ball, I'm standing poised and breathing.

Shoulders.

I'm not hitting the ball, I'm softening my jaw, letting the release flow into my shoulders, back and legs.

I'm not hitting the ball, I'm letting its image come into the back of my head.

I'm not hitting the ball, I'm seeing in my mind's eye on the left of my head where it's going to land. Shoulders.

I'm not hitting the ball, I'm releasing, breathing, soft jaw, ball in my eyes, spiral and ...*now*

Yes! There it goes. Nailed it!

I bring my knees back, stand tall and follow the arc and see it land right in the middle of my target. I can tell Ian's impressed, and I'm happy with the shot. I'd say that's about 140 yards to the front edge. Should be a fairly easy shot from there to get onto the green.

Now I've a gentle walk down the fairway and I can let my legs swing freely from my hips and sense a spring off the grass beneath my feet. Walk tall, long arms, long legs, release from the hips and let my lower legs swing through like pendulums on a clock. That's letting my lower back stay free from tension and I feel great.

Ian's ball landed about eight yards behind mine and slightly to the right. I stand tall and watch Ian play his next shot. It's not too bad. He's on the green, I reckon about five yards to the left of the flag but with a downward slope to the hole.

Okay, me again. I need a six-iron for this shot. I'll look to land this one at a spot to the right of the flag so I can putt uphill.

Nice and easy for the practice. No tension anywhere, great! That first shot and the walk down the fairway has loosened me up and

I feel good. Step forward to the ball. Think up, release and breathe. Soften jaw and shoulders and here we go.

Not exactly where I wanted it, just a yard or two to the left, but what the heck. I can still sink it from there.

It's getting warmer and the breeze has dropped. It's going to be a fine day. I'll enjoy my stroll to the green and see how Ian plays his shot.

Stand tall, breathe and enjoy the view.

Ian's ball stops just short of the hole and he taps in for a par.

Me again. It's just under six yards to the hole. No problem. Lined up, relax. Release up into my stance, jaw, shoulders and breathe. Practice stroke is good, nice pendulum action with no tension. Step up, feel the air going in and out of my nose. Still. Release and hear the club touch the ball and send it off nicely on target…. it's in! One under. Good start."

Okay we'll leave him there and let him get on with it.

All's Well That Ends Well

So there you have it. Tom can now approach the tee, check his jaw is relaxed, be aware of his ribs moving as he breathes, and get a sense of his toes in his socks and the ground under his feet as he assesses the situation. Tom's still not thinking about playing the shot as he walks to the tee. He's just sensing the ground under his feet. He can place his ball on the tee and think about how he bends his ankles, knees and hips to get down there. He can maintain awareness of his upper body and the touch of the club handle on his hands, as he releases his legs to go 'up' into his stance. Throughout this process he doesn't think about hitting the ball at any time. Even as he brings the club up, he's still not thinking of the ball because it would only cause him to stiffen up unnecessarily and prematurely.

I appreciate that some would say using the words '*I'm not hitting the ball.....*' will be translated by the unconscious mind as '*hitting the ball*', but while Tom is in the moment and fully aware of all his thoughts and actions, he can differentiate between the not hitting and hitting the ball part. Also notice how he has to think less about his body and what he's doing with it as he moves from being in the moment to getting into The Zone. Once there, it becomes a simpler game. He may slip out of it occasionally as he continues his round, but as long as he stays in the moment and doesn't become anxious, he'll find his way back.

So, to overcome the problem with his swing Tom has to first learn to 'stop' – to rediscover his natural poise and build a new set of efficient movement patterns away from his game. This enables him to reduce the level of activity in his nervous system to an appropriate minimum. With practice he can get into the moment and focus on his breathing, muscle tension and position before he's even picked up his club. He can now stay on the ball and 'see the stimulus coming' with great big bells on – something that would previously have caused him to tense his shoulders.

By maintaining a state of stillness and mindfulness, he can play the shot that has been there all along and he can minimise the errors. By combining a heightened sense of awareness with a new understanding of his body, he now feels more in control. His attention to detail relating to each action helps him get into the moment and drift more often into The Zone.

This has allowed him to consciously start to reduce the discrepancy between his intent and the actual outcome, in other words, develop his skill and build confidence.

So, to get into The Zone Tom has to:

- **Be in the moment by focusing on the activity in hand, whether he's walking, standing, going into his stance or preparing to take the shot.**

- **Be detached from the outcome.**

- **Keep his jaw, neck and shoulders relaxed.**

- **Sense the ground under his feet.**

- **Prevent his habitual reactions taking over.**

- **Enjoy the moment and let nature take its course.**

To do this he needs to practise every day, both on and off the course, but if he does this in the right frame of mind it won't seem like any effort at all.

This new approach will, over time, continue to change his concept of his body and how it can move. As his 'body sense' improves he'll get better at recognising unnecessary tension in his technique and he'll continue to reduce the small, previously imperceptible actions that would have interfered with his play. With his newfound ability he'll feel as if the wool has been pulled from his eyes, and his knowledge of his game will grow. By focusing on the non-golfing parts of his technique, that is, the way he uses his body to set himself up to play his shots, he can simplify his game by removing unnecessary actions and allow his body to flow freely.

Spiderman has his *spider sense* that tingles to warn him of imminent danger; Tom now has his *golf sense* to alert him to any inappropriate preparations he makes in anticipation of playing a shot. His new *golf sense* will continue to bring enjoyment and appreciation of his body and his game and, in the process, lower his handicap. Tom also has a big advantage over Spiderman because he's learned this skill and therefore won't lose it – so long as he uses it. Spiderman's ability was acquired by accident, and therefore he won't know how it works. And, of course, Tom doesn't have to wear a mask to conceal his identity – although he may have to conceal the big grin on his face that will give the game away!

Now it's your turn.

Ten Steps To Playing In The Zone

1) Practise the *Playing In The Zone* exercises in this book – see table on page 7.

2) Apply the techniques away from the course at first, i.e. on the range or at home.

3) Let your preparation feel different.

4) Be prepared to change your technique.

5) Practise being in the moment both on and off the course — see pages 111-115 (Getting Down To Business).

6) Keep an open mind and continue to experiment.

7) Take a course of lessons in The Alexander Technique — see useful resources on page 153.

8) Test different foods and note the effects on your performance. Consult a qualified nutritionist for professional guidance.

9) Treat yourself and invest in a set of custom-fit clubs to optimise your control and power.

10) Enjoy your golf.

Useful Resources

Further resources including audio instructions, videos and help on posture and sports injuries are available from my website at:-

www.play-better-golf.com

www.play-better-golf.com/resources.html (includes mp3 files)

You can keep up to date with my latest articles and ideas by following me on Twitter at

www.twitter.com/roy_palmer

Further information about some of the techniques and methods mentioned in this book is available from the websites below:

The Alexander Technique

www.stat.org.uk

www.alexandertechnique.com

Feldenkrais Method

www.feldenkrais.com

Podiatry/Golf Orthotics

www.feetforlife.org/foot_health/sports.html

www.footdynamics.com/performance_sports.htm

Also by Roy Palmer

Zone Mind, Zone Body
How to breakthrough to new levels of fitness
and performance – by doing less!

Ecademy Press Limited (October 2006)

The Performance Paradox
Challenging the conventional methods
of sports training and exercise

FrontRunner Publications (March 2001)

Lightning Source UK Ltd.
Milton Keynes UK
13 January 2011

165627UK00007B/64/P